LITTLE TALKS WITH GOD

PARACLETE POCKET CLASSICS

LITTLE TALKS WITH GOD

Catherine of Siena

PARACLETE PRESS
BREWSTER, MASSACHUSETTS

Little Talks with God

2007 First Printing

© 2007 by Paraclete Press, Inc.
ISBN 978-1-55725-531-0

**Library of Congress Cataloging-in-Publication Data as catalogued for
original Edition**
Catherine, of Siena, Saint, 1347–1380.
    Little talks with God / Catherine of Siena ; edited and mildly
modernized by Henry L. Carrigan, Jr.
        p. cm.
    Includes bibliographical references.
    ISBN 1-55725-272-6 (pbk.)
    1. Catherine, of Siena, Saint, 1347–1380. 2. Christian women
saints—Italy—Biography. 3. Spiritual life—Catholic Church. I.
Carrigan, Henry L., 1954– II. Title.
    BX4700.C4 A3 2001
    248.4'82—dc21   00-012922

10 9 8 7 6 5 4 3 2 1

Published by Paraclete Press
Brewster, Massachusetts
www.paracletepress.com

Printed in the United States of America.

CONTENTS

INTRODUCTION

O**N** O**CTOBER** 4, 1970, the Roman Catholic Church awarded the title of Doctor of the Church to two women: Teresa of Avila and Catherine of Siena. The writings and teachings of both these women remain very popular today, but it is Catherine's writings that teach us the most about incorporating our spiritual natures and our quests for union with God into our daily lives.

Although she is often called a mystic like Meister Eckhart, Catherine combined her own mystical experiences with a fervent activism. She was a Dominican, but she was not a cloistered member of that Order. Instead, from the very beginning she was active in ministering to the sick and aiding the poor. She also played a significant role in the politics of church and state in fourteenth-century Italy. Yet, in the midst of her activism, Catherine's quest for justice and equity was founded in her own experience of union with God. The knowledge and truth that she gained from this encounter strengthened her as she worked tirelessly to share God's love and compassion with those around her.

Catherine reached out to her society by writing her works in the language of the people rather than in the Latin of the Church. So popular were her books that they were some of the first to be brought into print. She had a devoted and large following among all classes of society in Siena, and they considered her their teacher.

Catherine was a prolific letter writer, but it is *The Dialogue*, titled *Little Talks with God* in this edition, that has brought her teachings to the widest audience. In it she offers a glimpse of the means whereby God's grace and mercy may be known in full knowledge and truth. *Little Talks with God* provides spiritual seekers a guidebook for incorporating the spiritual in the everyday.

Biography

Catherine was born in 1347, the twenty-fourth of twenty-five children. She was a headstrong and independent child, clever and ingenious in her religious devotion. Catherine's passionate desire for truth and the knowledge of God motivated her very being, even in her youth.

The Dominican Order influenced Catherine greatly. She often visited the church and cloister of San Domenico, a hub of Dominican teaching, spending a great deal of time with these teachers.

She was also influenced in Dominican teachings by the brother of her brother-in-law, Tommaso della Fonte, who had joined the Dominican Order in 1349.

Another group that impressed Catherine was a group of women in Siena known as the *Mantellate*. These women, who wore the habit of the Dominican Order, lived in their homes and ministered to the sick and poor. Even though they did not live in a cloister, they were directed by a prioress. By the time she was fourteen, Catherine had decided not to marry, and she sought and gained entrance to this group of women.

Raymond Capua, her earliest biographer and close friend, records that Catherine vowed her virginity to God when she was just seven years old. At fifteen, she defied her parents and refused their efforts to force her to marry, and at eighteen she obtained the habit. After she joined the Dominicans, she lived for a period of about three years in silence and solitude, leaving her room only to attend Mass. By the time she was twenty-one, she had experienced her "mystical espousal" to Christ.

Much like Mother Teresa, Catherine devoted herself to taking care of the sick and indigent.

However, she never gave up her contemplative life, and could often be found at home in her room teaching her followers about the Bible, theology, and God's grace.

In 1370, Catherine had one of her most profound mystical experiences—her "mystical death." For four hours she experienced ecstatic union with God, even though to outside observers she appeared to be dead. This experience led her to become more severe in her self-discipline, and enabled her to have a clear vision of the ways that she could introduce God's truth to the world.

Catherine worked tirelessly in political and religious affairs. In 1375, in Pisa, she preached that military strength could be best used to win unbelievers in the Holy Land. She preached that martyrdom for Christ was honorable, and so she supported a Crusade through her words. In the same year she received the stigmata, though by her own request these wounds were not visible.

Catherine soon became involved in urging Gregory XI to move the papacy from Avignon back to Rome. During these years she was also active in preaching about clergy reform. After Gregory's death, Urban VI replaced him as pope. Because many people opposed Urban when he was elected pope, Catherine foresaw the possibility that schism could occur in the Church. She began a furious letter-writing campaign in order to urge fidelity to the Church. Much of this urging makes its way into her writings.

From the time Catherine was thirty until her death at thirty-three, she directed a "household" in Siena where women and men lived by strict observance to poverty and alms. Her final years were filled with physical agony, even though she managed to attend services at St. Peter's each day. She died on April 29, 1380, and since 1969, the Roman Catholic Church has observed this day as her feast day.

These Little Talks

These conversations between Catherine and God explore in detail Catherine's own restless search for the truth that is God. According to *The Dialogue*, our ecstatic union with God teaches us the humility we need in order to know God as Truth and Love. Out of God's great love, we are enabled to love our neighbors with the love that God has for us. Nowhere is this better expressed than in the opening paragraph of these "little talks":

When the soul is lifted by a great, yearning desire for the honor of God and the salvation of souls, it practices the ordinary virtues and remains in the cell of self-knowledge, so that it may know better God's goodness toward it. It does this because knowledge must come before love, and only when it has attained love can it strive to follow and to clothe itself with the truth.

And loving, she seeks to pursue truth and clothe herself in it. Catherine's "little talks" provide us with a means whereby we can fold our own eager quest for God's love and truth into the many and busy pathways of our daily lives.

ON DIVINE
PROVIDENCE

*How a servant of God, elevated by her desire
for God's honor and for the salvation of her
neighbors, after she had seen the union of the
soul with God, exerted herself in humble
prayer and asked of God four requests.*

When the soul is lifted by a great, yearning
desire for the honor of God and the
salvation of souls, it practices the ordinary
virtues and remains in the cell of self-knowledge,
so that it may know better God's goodness
toward it. It does this because knowledge must
come before love, and only when it has attained
love can it strive to follow and to clothe itself
with the truth.

But humble and continuous prayer, founded
on knowledge of oneself and of God, is the best
way for the creature to receive such a taste of the
truth. Following the footprints of Christ crucified,
and through humble and unceasing prayer, the
soul is united with God. He remakes her in his
image through desire, affection, and union of

love. Christ seems to have meant this when he said: "Those who keep my commandments are the ones who love me, and I will reveal myself to them; they shall be one with me and I one with them." In several places we find similar words, by which we can see that the soul becomes another himself through the effect of love.

So you may see this more clearly, I will mention a story that a servant of God told me. When she was exalted in prayer, God did not conceal from her the love that he has for his servants. Instead, he revealed that love, saying to her, "Open the eye of your intellect and gaze into me, and you shall see the beauty of my rational creature. Look at those creatures whom I have created in my image and likeness, and have clothed with the wedding garment of love and adorned with many virtues, by which they are united with me through love. Yet if you should ask me who these are, I should reply," said the gentle and loving Word of God, "they are another me, for they have lost and denied their own will, and they are clothed, united, and conformed to my will." It is therefore true that the soul is united with God through love's affection.

So this servant of God, who wanted to know and follow the truth more faithfully, addressed four requests to the supreme and eternal Father. First, she prayed for herself, for this servant believed that she could not be an example to her neighbor in matters of doctrine and prayer if she did not first obtain her own virtue. Her second prayer was for the reformation of the holy church. The third was a general prayer for the entire world, particularly for the peace of Christians who rebel against and persecute the holy church. In the fourth prayer she asked for divine providence to sustain the world, and to be active in a certain case with which she was concerned.

How the soul's desire grew when
God showed her the world's need.

This servant's desire was great and continuous, but it grew even greater when the eternal Truth showed her the world's neediness and its tempestuous offenses against God.

She understood this matter even better from a letter she received from her spiritual father, in which he explained to her the pain and sadness caused by such offenses against God, the loss of soul, and the persecutions against the holy church. This knowledge inflamed her holy desire with grief over the offenses against God. She anticipated joyously that God would provide against such great evils. She looked forward to morning's arrival in order to hear Mass. In such communion, the soul binds itself firmly to God, and knows better his truth, since the soul is then in God and God in the soul.

When the hour of Mass arrived in the morning— it was the feast day of Mary—she anxiously sought her usual place. From a deep knowledge of herself and with a feeling of holy justice, she was ashamed of her own imperfection, for it seemed to be the cause of all the world's evils. In this knowledge, she cleansed the stains covering her guilty soul, saying: "Eternal Father, I accuse myself before you, so that you may punish me for my sins in this life. Since my sins cause my neighbor to suffer, I beg you, in your mercy, to punish me for them."

How very pleasing to God is the willing desire to suffer for Him.

"The willing desire to bear every pain, even death, for the salvation of souls is very pleasing to me. The more the soul endures, the more it shows that it loves me. By loving me, it comes to know more of my truth. The more it knows, the more pain and intolerable grief it feels at the sins committed by others against me.

"You asked me to sustain you and to punish the faults of others in you. You did not say that you were really asking for love, light, and knowledge of the truth. I have already told you that as love increases so do grief and pain. Those of you who grow in love also grow in sadness. I say to you all, if you ask, I will give it to you, for I do not deny anything to the one who asks of me in truth.

"The love of divine charity is so closely joined in the soul with perfect patience that neither can leave the soul without the other. If the soul chooses to love me, it should choose also to endure pains for me in whatever way that I send them. Patience cannot be proved in any way other than suffering, and patience is united with love.

"Have courage, for, unless you do, you will not prove yourselves to be spouses of my Truth, and faithful children, nor of the company of those who relish the taste of my honor, and the salvation of souls."

How every virtue and every defect is obtained by means of our neighbor.

"You achieve every virtue and every defect by means of your neighbor. Those who hate me, therefore, injure their neighbor and therefore themselves, who are their own chief neighbors. This injury is both general and particular. It is general, because you are obliged to love your neighbor as yourself. Because you love your neighbor, you should help him spiritually, through prayer and by counseling her with words. Assist him spiritually and temporally with your good will, according to his needs.

"A person who does not love does not help his neighbor, and thus harms himself. She cuts himself off from grace, and harms his neighbor by depriving him of the benefit of the prayers and sweet desires he is bound to offer to me for his neighbor. Every act of help he performs should proceed from the compassion he has because of his love for me.

"Every evil is also done by means of your neighbor. If you do not love me, you cannot have compassion for your neighbor. Thus, all evils derive from the soul's lack of love for me and his neighbor. Since this person does no good, it follows that he must do evil.

"Against whom does he commit evil? First to himself and then to his neighbor. But not against me, for no evil can touch me, except insofar as I count that evil he does to himself as evil done to me. He harms himself through sin, which deprives the neighbor of grace. He hurts his neighbor by not paying him the debt of love that he owes his neighbor. He ought to help his neighbor through the prayer and holy desire he offers to me on the neighbor's behalf.

"This assistance is owed to every rational creature. But such help is more useful when it is offered to those close at hand. You are all compelled to help one another by word, doctrine, good works, and in other respects that in which your neighbor may be in need. You should counsel your neighbor exactly as you would counsel yourselves, without any self-love. The person who does not love God does not do this because he has no love toward his neighbor. By not loving God, he does the neighbor a special harm. He does the neighbor evil, not just by not doing the good he might do him, but by doing him positive harm.

"In this way, sin causes a physical and mental injustice. The mental injustice happens as soon as the sinner enjoys the idea of sin, hates virtue, and takes pleasure in sensual self-love, which deprives him of the affection of love that he should have toward me and his neighbor. He then commits one sin after another against his neighbor, according to the various ways that please his perverse, sensual will. Sometimes he engages in cruelty.

"It is general cruelty to see oneself and other creatures in danger of death and damnation, and to do nothing because of lack of grace. The sinner is so cruel that he does not help himself or others by loving virtue and hating vice. He might even want to be crueler by playing the devil and tempting others to forsake virtue and embrace vice. This is spiritual cruelty, for he makes himself the instrument of destroying life and dealing out death.

"Bodily cruelty originates in greed. This cruelty not only hampers a person from helping his neighbor, but also causes him to seize things that belong to others. Sometimes he does this by the arbitrary use of power. Other times it is accomplished through cheating and fraud. He often forces his neighbor to recover his own goods, and sometimes his own body.

"This miserable vice of cruelty will eventually deprive the one who practices it of all my mercy, unless he practices kindness and compassion toward his neighbor! Sometimes he produces insults, and murder often follows them. He often defiles others and becomes a stinking beast, poisoning not only one or two, but everyone who approaches in love or fellowship.

"If a proud person holds a position of authority, he also produces injustice and cruelty. Whom does pride hurt? Your neighbors. You injure them when, in your opinion of yourself, you make yourself superior to them and look down on them.

"Dearest daughter, grieve over offenses committed against me, and weep over these dead ones, so that, by prayer, the bands of their death may be loosened! Notice how in every kind of person and in every society, sin is always committed against one's neighbor, for there is no sin that does not touch others. You commit a secret sin when you deny your neighbor the things you should give her. You commit an open sin when you perform positive acts of sin.

"It is thus true that every sin committed against me is done by means of your neighbors."

*How our relationships with our neighbors
lead us to virtue, and why it is that
virtues differ in every person*

"I have told you how negative relationships with our neighbors lead to all sins, because we deprive people of the respect of love, which gives light to every virtue. In the same way, self-love, which destroys love and compassion toward the neighbor, is the principle and foundation of every evil. All scandals, hatred, cruelty, and every sort of trouble issue from this perverse root of self-love. Such distorted self-love has poisoned the entire world, and has weakened the mystical body of the holy church and the universal body of the believers in the Christian religion. Therefore, all virtues grow out of the degree to which we love our neighbors. Indeed, love and compassion give life to all virtues. No virtue can be attained without compassion, which is the pure love of me.

"When the soul knows itself, it finds humility and hates its own sensual passion. It learns the perverse law that is part of her body and that always battles against its spirit. It begins to hate its own sensuality, fervently crushing it under the heel of reason. Then it discovers in itself the bounty of my goodness, because of the many benefits that I have given it. It then ponders these things in itself.

"In its humility, the soul attributes to me the knowledge of itself it has obtained. It knows that, by my grace, I have delivered it from darkness and lifted it up into the light of true knowledge.

"When the soul knows my goodness, it loves it both with and without a mediator. It loves it even without placing itself as mediator, or any other to its own advantage. But virtue is a mediator that it has conceived through its love of me. It sees that it can only become grateful and acceptable to me by hating sin and loving virtue. When the soul conceives virtue through loving compassion, it bears the fruit of virtue to its neighbor. It cannot act out the truth it has conceived in itself in any other way. It can only love me in truth, and in the same truth it serves its neighbor.

"And it cannot be otherwise, because love of me and of one's neighbor are one and the same thing; and, so far as the soul loves me, it loves its neighbor, because love towards one's neighbor issues from me. This is the means which I have given you, so that you may exercise and prove your virtue; because, inasmuch as you can do me no profit, you should do good to your neighbor. This proves that you possess me by grace in your soul, producing much fruit for your neighbor and making prayers to me, as you seek with sweet and loving desire my honor and the salvation of souls.

"The soul, enamored of my truth, never ceases to serve the whole world in general, and more or less in a particular case according to the disposition of the recipient and the ardent desire of the donor. For the endurance of suffering alone, without desire, is not sufficient to punish a fault.

"When the soul has discovered the advantage of this unitive love in me, by means of which it truly loves itself, extending its desire to the salvation of the whole world and thus coming to the aid of the world's neediness, it strives to fix its eye on the needs of its neighbor in particular.

"Therefore, it helps those who are at hand, according to the various graces which I have entrusted to it to administer. One it helps with doctrine, that is, with words, giving sincere counsel without any respect of persons. Another with the example of a good life. Thus, indeed, all give to their neighbor the edification of a holy and honorable life.

"These are the virtues, along with many others too many to enumerate, which are brought forth in the love of one's neighbor. But, although I have given them in such a different way, that is to say not all to one, but one virtue to one, and another to another, it so happens that it is impossible to have one without having them all, because all the virtues are bound together.

"Learn, therefore, that in many cases I give one virtue to be the chief of the others. That is to say, to one I will give principally love, to another principally justice, to another principally humility, or a lively faith, or prudence, or temperance, or patience, or fortitude. I could easily have created men possessed of all that they should need both for body and soul, but I desire that one should have need of the other, and that they should be my ministers to administer the graces and the gifts that they have received from me.

"Whether man desires to or not, he cannot help making an act of love. It is true, however, that that act, unless made through love of me, profits him nothing so far as grace is concerned. See then, that I have made men my ministers, and have placed them in differing stations and various ranks, in order that they may make use of the virtue of love.

"Therefore, I show you that in my house are many mansions, and that I wish for no other thing than love. For in the love of me is fulfilled and completed the love of one's neighbor, and the law is observed. For only those who are bound to me with this love can be of use in their state of life."

ON DISCRETION

A parable showing how love, humility, and discretion are united; and how the soul should conform itself to this parable.

"Do you know how the three virtues of love, humility, and discretion stand together? It is as if a circle were drawn on the surface of the earth, and a tree, with an offshoot joined to its side, grew in the center of the circle. The tree is nourished in the earth contained in the diameter of the circle, for if the tree were out of the earth, it would die and give no fruit.

"Now, consider, in the same way, that the soul is a tree existing by love, and that it can live by nothing else than love. And consider that if this soul does not have in very truth the divine love of perfect charity, it cannot produce fruit of life, but only of death.

"It is necessary then, that the root of this tree, that is the affection of the soul, should grow in, and issue from, the circle of true self-knowledge which is contained in me, who have neither beginning nor end, like the circumference of the circle. Turn as you will within a circle, inasmuch as the circumference has neither end nor beginning, you always remain within it.

"This knowledge of yourself and of me is found in the earth of true humility, which is as wide as the diameter of the circle, that is, as wide as the knowledge of self and of me. Otherwise, the circle would not be without an end and a beginning. It would have its beginning in knowledge of self, and its end in confusion, if this knowledge were not contained in me.

"Thus, the tree of love feeds on humility, bringing forth from its side the offshoot of true discretion, from the heart of the tree. And true discretion is the affection of love in the soul, and the patience, proving that I am in the soul and the soul in me.

"This tree then, so sweetly planted, produces fragrant blossoms of virtue, with many scents of great variety, inasmuch as the soul renders the fruit of grace and of usefulness to its neighbor, according to the zeal of those who come to receive fruit from my servants. And to me it renders the sweet odor of glory and praise to my name, and so fulfills the object of its creation.

"In this way, therefore, the soul reaches the end and goal of its being, that is myself, its God, who am eternal Life. And these fruits cannot be taken

from it without its will, inasmuch as they are all flavored with discretion, because they are all united."

*How penance and other corporal exercises are
instruments for arriving at virtue, and not the
principal affection of the soul;
and how the light of discretion shines in
various other ways.*

"*T*hese are the fruits and the works that I
seek from the soul, namely, the proving of
virtue in the time of need. And yet some time
ago, when you wanted to do great penance for
my sake, and asked, 'What can I do to endure
suffering for You, Lord?' I replied to you, 'I take
delight in few words and many works.'

"I wished to show you that one who merely
calls on me with the sound of words, saying:
'Lord, Lord, I want to do something for you,'
and one, who desires for my sake to mortify his
body with many penances, and not his own *will*,
did not give me much pleasure. Instead, I desire
the manifold works of endurance with patience,
together with the other virtues intrinsic to the
soul, all of which must be active in order to
obtain fruits worthy of grace.

"All other works, founded on any other principle
than this, I judge to be mere words. They are

finite works, and I, who am infinite, seek infinite works, that is, an infinite perfection of love.

"I wish therefore that the works of penance and of other corporal exercises should be observed merely as means to an end, and not as the fundamental affection of the soul. For, if the principal affection of the soul were placed in penance, I should receive a finite thing like a word. Once a word has issued from the mouth, it is no more—unless it has issued with affection of the soul, which conceives and brings forth virtue in truth. In other words, it is no more unless the finite operation, which I have called a word, should be joined with affection or love, in which case it would be pleasing to me.

"And this is because such a work would not be alone, but accompanied by true discretion, using corporal works as means, and not as the principal foundation. For it would not be becoming that the principal foundation should be placed in penance only, or in any exterior corporal act; such works are finite, since they are done in finite time. It is often profitable for the creature to omit them, and even for it to be made to do so.

"Therefore, when the soul omits these works through necessity, being unable through various circumstances to complete an action that it has begun, or, as may frequently happen, through obedience at the order of its director, it is well. Indeed, if it continued then to do them, it not only would receive no merit, but would offend me. So you see that they are merely finite. Therefore, the soul ought to adopt them as a means, and not as an end. For, if it takes them as an end it will be obliged, some time or other, to leave them, and will then remain empty.

"This, my trumpeter, the glorious Paul, taught you when he said in his epistle that you should mortify the body and destroy self-will, knowing how to keep a rein on the body and to macerate the flesh whenever it wishes to combat the spirit. But the will should be dead and annihilated in everything, and subject to my will.

"And this slaying of the will, the virtue of discretion renders to the soul as its due. Discretion brings to the soul hatred and disgust of its own offenses and sensuality, which hatred it has acquired by self-knowledge. This is the knife that slays and cuts off all self-love founded in self-will. These then are the ones who give me not only words but manifold works, and in these I take delight.

"And then I said that I desired few words, and many actions. By the use of the word 'many,' I assign no particular number to you. That is, because the affection of the soul, founded in love, which gives life to all the virtues and good works, should increase infinitely. And yet by this I do not exclude words. I merely said that I wished few of them, showing you that every actual operation, as such, is finite, and therefore I called them of little account. But they please me when they are performed as the instruments of virtue, and not as a principal end in themselves.

"However, no one should judge that he has achieved greater perfection, because he performs great penances and gives himself in excess to the slaying of his body, than one who does less. For neither virtue nor merit consists in excess. Otherwise he would be in an evil state, who, for some legitimate reason, was unable to do actual penance. Merit consists in the virtue of love alone, flavored with the light of true discretion, without which the soul is worth nothing. And this love should be directed to me endlessly, boundlessly, since I am the supreme and eternal Truth.

"The soul can therefore place neither laws nor limits to its love for me. But its love for its neighbor, on the contrary, is limited by certain conditions. The light of discretion (which proceeds from love) gives to the neighbor a conditioned love. Such a love, being ordered aright, does not cause the injury of sin to self in order to be useful to others. For, if one single sin were committed to save the whole world from hell, or to obtain one great virtue, the motive would not be a rightly ordered or discreet love, but rather indiscreet. For it is not lawful to perform even one act of great virtue and profit to others by means of the guilt of sin.

"Holy discretion ordains that the soul should direct all its powers to my service with a manly zeal. It should love its neighbor with such devotion that it would lay down a thousand times, if it were possible, the life of its body for the salvation of souls. It should endure pains and torments so that its neighbor may have the life of grace, and give its temporal substance for the profit and relief of his body.

"This is the supreme office of discretion, which proceeds from charity. So you see how discreetly every soul who wishes for grace should pay its debts. That is, it should love me with an infinite love and without measure. But it should love its neighbor with measure, with a restricted love, not doing itself the injury of sin in order to be useful to others.

"This is St. Paul's counsel to you, when he says that charity ought to be concerned first with self, otherwise it will never be of perfect usefulness to others. And this is because, when perfection is not in the soul, everything the soul does for itself and for others is imperfect.

"It would not, therefore, be just that creatures, who are finite and created by me, should be saved through an offense done to me, the infinite Good. The more serious the fault is in such a case, the less fruit will the action produce. Therefore, in no way should you ever incur the guilt of sin.

"And this true love knows well, because it carries with itself the light of holy discretion, that light that dissipates all darkness. Discretion takes away ignorance and is the condiment of every instrument of virtue. Holy discretion is a prudence that cannot be cheated, a fortitude that cannot be beaten, a perseverance from end to end. It stretches from heaven to earth, that is, from knowledge of me to knowledge of self, and from love of me to love of others.

"The soul escapes dangers by its true humility. By its prudence it flies from all the nets of the world and its creatures. With unarmed hands, that is, through much endurance, it discomfits the devil and the flesh with this sweet and glorious light. By this light of discretion, it knows its own fragility, and it renders to its weakness its due of hatred.

"Therefore the soul has trampled on the world, and placed it under the feet of her affection, despising it and holding it vile, and thus becoming lord of it. And the fools of the world cannot take the virtues from such a soul. Indeed, all their persecutions increase its virtues and prove them. These virtues are first conceived by the virtue of love, and then are proved through one's neighbor, bringing forth their fruit on him.

"Thus if virtue were not visible and did not shine in the time of trial, it would show that it was not truly conceived. Perfect virtue cannot exist and give fruit except by means of one's neighbor, even as a woman who has conceived a child, if she does not bring it forth so that it may appear before the eyes of all, deprives her husband of his fame of paternity. It is the same with me, the Spouse of the soul; if the soul does not produce its child of virtue in its love for its neighbor, showing its child to those in need, in truth, it has not conceived virtue at all. And this is also true of the vices, all of which are committed by means of the neighbor."

*How this servant of God grew by
means of the divine response, and how
her sorrows grew less; and how she
prayed to God for the holy church,
and for her own people.*

Then that servant of God thirsted and burned with the very great desire that she had conceived on learning the inexpressible love of God, as shown in his great goodness. Seeing the breadth of his charity, that, with such sweetness, he had deigned to reply to her request and to satisfy it, gave hope to her sorrow on account of offenses against God and the damage of the holy church. This sight diminished, and yet, at the same time, increased her sorrow.

For the supreme and eternal Father, in manifesting the way of perfection, showed her anew her own guilt and the loss of souls. Because of the knowledge that this servant had obtained of herself, she knew more of God. Knowing the goodness of God in herself, the sweet mirror of God, she knew her own dignity and indignity. Her dignity was that of her creation in the image of God, and this dignity was given her by grace, and not as her due.

In that same mirror of the goodness of God, this servant knew her own indignity, which was the consequence of her own fault. Just as one more readily sees spots on one's face by looking in a mirror, so the soul that, with true knowledge of self, rises with desire and gazes with the eye of the intellect at itself in the sweet mirror of God, knows better the stains of its own face by the purity which it sees in him.

Therefore, because light and knowledge increased in that servant, a sweet sorrow grew in her. At the same time, her sorrow was diminished by the hope that the supreme Truth gave her. As fire grows when it is fed with wood, so the fire grew in that soul, to such an extent that it was no longer possible for her body to endure it without the departure of her soul. Had she not been surrounded by the strength of him who is the supreme Strength, it would not have been possible for her to have lived any longer.

This servant then, being purified by the fire of divine love, which she found in the knowledge of herself and of God, and by her hunger for the salvation of the whole world, and for the reformation of the holy church, grew in her hope of obtaining her desires. Therefore she rose with confidence before the supreme Father and showed him the leprosy of the holy church and the misery of the world, saying, as if with the words of Moses, "Lord, turn the eyes of your mercy upon your people, and upon the mystical body of the holy church, for you will be the more glorified if you pardon so many creatures and give them the light of knowledge. For all will render you praise when they see themselves escape through your infinite goodness from the clouds of mortal sin, and from eternal damnation. Then you will be praised not only by my wretched self, who has so much offended you, and who is the cause and the instrument of all this evil.

"Therefore I pray your divine and eternal love to take your revenge on me, and to do mercy to your people. Never will I depart from before your presence until I see that you grant them mercy.

"For what is it to me if I have life, and your people death, and the clouds of darkness cover your bride, the church, when it is my own sins, and not those of your other creatures, that are the principal cause of this? I desire, then, and beg of you, by your grace, that you have mercy on your people. I adjure you to do this by your uncreated love, which moved you to create man in your image and likeness, saying, 'Let us make man in our own image,' And you did this, eternal Trinity, so that mankind might participate in everything belonging to you, the most high and eternal Trinity.

"Therefore you gave us memory, in order to receive your benefits, by which we participate in the power of the eternal Father. You gave us intellect, that he might know, seeing your goodness, and might participate in the wisdom of your only-begotten Son. And you gave us will, that we might love that which our intellect has seen and known of your truth, and thus participate in the clemency of your Holy Spirit.

"What reason did you have for creating man in such dignity? It was the inestimable love with which you saw your creature in yourself, and became enamored of him. For you created him through love, and destined him to be such that he might taste and enjoy your eternal Good. I see, therefore, that through his sin he lost this dignity in which you originally placed him, and by his rebellion against you, fell into a state of war with your kindness, that is to say, we all became your enemies.

"Therefore, moved by that same fire of love with which you created him, you willingly gave man a means of reconciliation, so that after the great rebellion into which he had fallen, there should come a great peace. And so you gave him the only-begotten Word, your Son, to be the mediator between us and you. He was our Justice, for he took on himself all our offenses and injustices, and performed your obedience, eternal Father, which you imposed on him when you clothed him with our humanity, our human nature, and our likeness.

"Oh, abyss of love! What heart can help breaking when it sees such dignity as yours descend to such lowliness as our humanity? We are your image, and you have become ours, by this union which you have accomplished with man, veiling the eternal Deity with the cloud of woe and the corrupted clay of Adam. For what reason?— Love. Therefore, you, God, have become man, and man has become God. By this inexpressible love of yours, therefore, I constrain you, and implore you, that you show mercy to your creatures."

How sin is more gravely punished after the passion of Christ than before; and how God promises to show mercy to the world and to the holy church, by means of the prayers and sufferings of his servants.

" *I* wish you to know, my daughter, that, although I have re-created and restored the human race to the life of grace through the blood of my only-begotten Son, men are not grateful. They go from bad to worse and from guilt to guilt, even persecuting me with many injuries. They take so little account of the graces that I have given them, and continue to give them, that, not only do they not attribute to grace what they have received, but they believe themselves on occasion to receive injuries from me, as if I desired anything else than their sanctification.

"I say to you that they will be more hard-hearted, and worthy of more punishment, and will, indeed, be punished more severely, now that they have received redemption in the blood of my Son, than they would have been before that redemption took place—that is, before the stain of Adam's sin was taken away. It is right that he who receives more should give more back, and should be under great obligation to him from whom he receives more.

"Man, then, was closely bound to me through his being, which I gave him, creating him in my own image and likeness. For that reason he was bound to render me glory; but he deprived me of it, and wished to give it to himself. Thus he came to transgress my obedience imposed on him, and became my enemy. And I destroyed his pride with my humility, humiliating the divine nature and taking your humanity. And freeing you from the service of the devil, I made you free.

"Not only did I give you liberty, but if you will examine, you will see that man has become God and God has become man, through the union of the divine with the human nature. This is the debt that men have incurred—the treasure of the Blood, by which they have been procreated to grace.

"See, therefore, how much more they owe after the redemption than before. They are now obliged to render me glory and praise by following in the steps of my incarnate Word, my only-begotten Son, for then they repay me the debt of love both of myself and of their neighbor, with true and genuine virtue. And if they do not do it, the greater will be their debt, and the greater will be the offense they fall into. Therefore, by divine justice, the greater will be their suffering in eternal damnation.

"A false Christian is punished more than a pagan, and the deathless fire of divine justice consumes him more, that is, afflicts him more. In his affliction, he feels himself being consumed by the worm of conscience, though, in truth, he is not consumed, because the damned do not lose their being through any torment that they receive. Therefore I say to you that they ask for death and cannot have it, for they cannot lose their being. The existence of grace they lose, through their fault, but not their natural existence.

"Therefore, guilt is more gravely punished after the redemption of the Blood than before, because man received more. But sinners neither seem to perceive this, nor to pay any attention to their own sins. And so they become my enemies, though I have reconciled them by means of the blood of my Son.

"But there is a remedy with which I appease my wrath—that is, by means of my servants, if they are jealous to constrain me by their desire. You see, therefore, that you have bound me with this bond which I have given you, because I wished to show mercy to the world.

"Therefore I give my servants hunger and desire for my honor, and the salvation of souls, so that, constrained by their tears, I may mitigate the fury of my divine justice. Therefore, take your tears and your sweat, drawn from the fountain of my divine love, and with them, wash the face of my bride, the church.

"I promise you that, by this means, my bride's beauty will be restored to her, not by the knife nor by cruelty, but peacefully, by humble and continued prayer, by the sweat and the tears shed by the fiery desire of my servants. Thus will I fulfill your desire, if you, on your part, endure much, and cast the light of your patience into the darkness of perverse man. Do not fear the world's persecutions, since I will protect you. My providence shall never fail you in the slightest need."

How, the road to heaven being broken through the disobedience of Adam, but God made of his Son a bridge by which man could pass.

"I have told you that I have made a bridge of my Word, my only-begotten Son, and this is the truth. I wish for you, my children, to know that the road was broken by the sin and disobedience of Adam, in such a way that no one could arrive at eternal life. Therefore men did not render me glory in the way in which they ought to have, as they did not participate in that good for which I had created them, and my truth was not fulfilled.

"This truth is that I have created man in my own image and likeness, so that he might have eternal life, and might partake of me, and taste my supreme and eternal sweetness and goodness.

But after sin had closed heaven and bolted the doors of mercy, the soul of man produced thorns and prickly brambles, and my creature found in himself rebellion against himself.

"The flesh immediately began to war against the spirit, and losing the state of innocence, it became a foul animal. Then all created things rebelled against man, whereas they would have been obedient to him if he had remained in the state in which I had placed him. But not remaining in that state, he transgressed my obedience, and became worthy of eternal death in soul and body.

"As soon as he had sinned, there arose a tempestuous flood, which continues to buffet him with its waves, bringing him weariness and trouble from himself, the devil, and the world. Everyone was drowned in the flood, because no one, with his own righteousness alone, could arrive at eternal life. And so, wishing to remedy your great evils, I have given you the bridge of my Son, so that you may pass across the flood—the tempestuous sea of this dark life—and not be drowned. See, therefore, under what obligation the creature is to me, and how ignorant he is not to take the remedy which I have offered, but to be willing to drown."

How God induces the soul to look at the greatness
of this bridge, which reaches from earth to heaven.

"Open, my daughter, the eye of your intellect, and you will see the accepted and the ignorant, the imperfect, and also the perfect who follow me in truth, so that you may grieve over the damnation of the ignorant, and rejoice over the perfection of my beloved servants.

"You will see further how those who walk in the light carry themselves, and how those who walk in the darkness carry themselves. I also want you to look at the bridge of my only-begotten Son and see its greatness. That is, that by it the earth of your humanity is joined to the greatness of the Deity, for it reaches from heaven to earth. I say then that this bridge constitutes the union which I have made with man.

"This bridge was necessary, in order to reform the road that was broken, so that man could pass through the bitterness of the world and arrive at life. But the bridge could not be made of sufficient earth to span the flood and give you eternal life, because the earth of human nature was not sufficient to remove the stain of Adam's sin, which corrupted the whole human race and gave out a stench.

"Therefore, it was necessary to join human nature with the height of my nature, the eternal Deity, making it sufficient to satisfy for the whole human race. Only in this way could human nature sustain the punishment, and the divine nature, united with the human, could make acceptable the sacrifice of my only Son, offered to me to take death from you and to give you life.

"So the loftiness of the divinity, humbled to the earth and joined with your humanity, made the bridge and re-formed the road. Why was this done? So that man might come to his true happiness with the angels. Observe, however, that it is not enough that my Son made you this bridge so that you could have life, unless you are willing to walk on it."

How this servant, wondering at the mercy of God, relates many gifts and graces given to the human race.

Then this servant, like an intoxicated person, could not contain herself. Standing before the face of God, she exclaimed, "How great is the eternal mercy with which you cover the sins of your creatures! I do not wonder that you say of those who abandon mortal sin and return to you, 'I do not remember that you have ever offended me.' Inexpressible mercy! No wonder you say to the converted, speaking of those who persecute you, 'I want you to pray for so-and-so, in order that I may show them mercy.'

"Mercy, you proceed from your eternal Father; divinity, with your power you govern the whole world: By you we were created, in you were we re-created in the blood of your Son. Your mercy preserves us; your mercy caused your Son to do battle for us, hanging by his arms on the wood of the cross, life and death battling together. Then life confounded the death of our sin, and the death of our sin destroyed the bodily life of the immaculate Lamb. Which one was finally conquered? Death! By what means? Mercy!

"Your mercy gives light and life. By it your clemency is known in all your creatures, both the just and the unjust. In the height of heaven your mercy shines in your saints. If I turn to the earth, it abounds with your mercy. In the darkness of hell your mercy shines, for the damned do not receive the pains they deserve; you temper justice with your mercy. By mercy you have washed us in the Blood, and by mercy you desire to converse with your creatures.

"Loving Madman! Was it not enough for you to take on human flesh, that you must also die? Was not death enough, that you must also descend into limbo, taking out of it the holy fathers, in order to fulfill your mercy and your truth in them? Because your goodness promises a reward to those who serve you in truth, you descended to limbo, in order to withdraw your servants from their pain and to give them the fruit of their labors.

"Your mercy constrains you to give even more to mortals, namely, to leave yourself to them in food. In this way we weak ones have comfort, and the ignorant, by commemorating you, do not lose the memory of your benefits.

"For this reason, every day you give yourself to man, representing yourself in the sacrament of the altar, in the body of your holy church. What has done this? Your mercy. Oh, divine mercy! My heart suffocates in thinking of you, for everywhere I turn my thoughts, I find nothing but mercy. Eternal Father! Forgive my ignorance that makes me presume to chatter to you. The love of your mercy will be my excuse before the face of your loving-kindness."

After this servant had refreshed her heart in the mercy of God by these words, she humbly waited for the fulfillment of the promise made to her. Then God continued his discourse:

"Dearest daughter, you have spoken to me of my mercy, because I gave it to you to taste and to see in the word I spoke to you: 'These are the ones for whom I plead with you to intercede with me.' But know that my mercy is beyond comprehension, far more than you can see, because your sight is imperfect, but my mercy is perfect and infinite. So there can be no relating between the two except what relating there may be between a finite and an infinite thing.

"But I have desired you to taste this mercy and also the dignity of mankind so that you might know better the cruelty of those wicked ones who travel below the bridge. Open the eye of your intellect, and wonder at those who drown themselves voluntarily. Wonder at the baseness to which they are fallen through their fault. For first they become weak and conceive mortal sin in their minds, and they then bring it forth and lose the life of grace. Just as a corpse can have no feeling or movement of itself, so those who are drowned in the stream of disordinate love of the world and of themselves are dead to the feeling and movement of grace.

"Because they are dead to grace, their memory takes no notice of my mercy. The eye of their intellect neither sees nor knows my truth. And their will is dead to my will, because it loves nothing but dead things. Since these three powers are dead, namely, the memory, the intellect, and the will, all the soul's operations both in deed and thought are dead as far as grace is concerned. For the soul cannot defend herself against its enemies, nor help itself through its own power, but only inasmuch as it is helped by me and my grace.

"Freewill, which remains as long as the mortal body lives, is the only thing remaining in this corpse. So it is true that every time this corpse asks for my help, he can have it, but never can he help himself. He has become intolerable to himself. He wants to govern the world, but is governed by that which is not, that is by sin, for in itself sin is nothing. Such people have become the servants and slaves of sin. I have made them trees of love with the life of grace, which they received in holy baptism. But they have become trees of death, because they are dead.

"Do you know how these trees find such roots of death? In the loftiness of pride, nourished by their own sensitive self-love. Their branches are their own impatience and its offshoot, indiscretion.

These, then, are the four principal vices that destroy the soul of those who are trees of death, because they have not drawn life from grace: pride, self-love, impatience, and indiscretion.

"Inside the tree the worm of conscience is nourished. But while man lives in mortal sin, the conscience is blinded by self-love, and therefore is felt but little. The fruits of this tree are mortal, for instead of drawing their nourishment from humility, they have drawn it from the roots of pride. Thus the miserable soul is full of ingratitude, from which proceeds every evil. If the soul were grateful for the benefits it has received, it would know me. Knowing me, it would know itself, and so would remain in my love. But the soul, as if blind, goes groping down the river, and it does not see that the water does not support it."

*Of the words that Christ said: "I will
send the Holy Spirit, who will rebuke
the world of injustice and of false judgment";
and how the first of these rebukes is continuous.*

"*T*here are three rebukes of injustice and false judgment. One was given when the Holy Spirit came upon the disciples. They, being fortified by my power and illuminated by the wisdom of my beloved Son, received all in the fullness of the Holy Spirit. The Holy Spirit, who is one with me and with my Son, rebuked the world, through the mouth of the apostles, with the doctrine of my Truth. They and all others who are descended from them, following the truth which they understand through the same means, reprove the world.

"This is that continuous rebuke that I make to the world by means of the Holy Scriptures and by my servants. I put the Holy Spirit on their tongues to announce my truth, even as the devil puts himself on the tongues of his servants, that is, on the tongues of those who pass through the river in iniquity. This is the sweet rebuke that I have fixed forever out of my great love for the salvation of souls. And they cannot say, 'I had no one who rebuked me,' because the truth is revealed to them, and it shows them vice and virtue.

"I have made men see the fruit of virtue and the hurtfulness of vice, to give them love and holy fear so they may hate vice and love virtue. And this truth has not been shown them by an angel, so they cannot say, 'The angel is a blessed spirit who cannot offend, and does not feel the vexations of the flesh as we do, nor the heaviness of our body.' No, it was in your mortal flesh that I gave the incarnate Word of my Truth.

"Who were the others who followed this Word? Mortal creatures, susceptible to pain like you, having the same opposition of the flesh to the spirit. Among them were the glorious Paul, my standard-bearer, and many other saints. By one thing or another they were tormented with torments that I permitted so that grace and virtue might increase in their souls. They were born in sin like you, and were nourished with similar food.

"I am God now as then. My power is not weakened, and cannot become weak. Therefore I can and will help those who want me to help them. Men show that they want my help when they come out of the river and walk by the bridge, following the doctrine of my Truth.

"Therefore no one has any excuse, because both rebukes and truth are constantly given to them. As a result, if they do not change their lives while they have time, they will be condemned by the second condemnation that will take place at the extremity of death. Then my justice will cry to them, 'Rise, you dead, and come to judgment!' In other words, 'You who are dead to grace and have reached the moment of your corporal death, rise and come before the supreme Judge with your injustice and false judgment. Come with the extinguished light of faith, which you received burning in holy baptism (and which you have blown out by the wind of pride). Come with the vanity of your heart, by which you set your sails to winds that were contrary to your salvation. For with the wind of self-esteem, you filled the sail of self-love.'

"In this way you hastened down the stream of the delights and dignities of the world by your own will. You followed your fragile flesh and the temptations of the devil, who, with the sail of your self-love and self-will set, has led you along the underway, which is a running stream, and so has brought you with himself to eternal damnation."

Of the second rebuke of injustice and false judgment, in general and in particular.

"This second rebuke, dearest daughter, is indeed a condemnation, for the soul has arrived at the end, where there can be no remedy. It is at the extremity of death, where it finds the worm of conscience, which I told you was blinded self-love. Now at the time of death, since it cannot get out of my hands, it begins to see, and therefore it is gnawed with remorse that its own sin has brought it into so great evil.

"But if the soul has light to know and grieve for its fault, not on account of the pain of hell that follows upon it, but on account of pain at her offense against me, who am supreme and eternal Good, still it can find mercy. However, if it passes the bridge of death alone and without light, with the worm of conscience and without the hope of the Blood, and bewails itself more on account of its first condemnation than on account of my displeasure, it arrives at eternal damnation.

"Then it is that my justice rebukes the soul cruelly of injustice and of false judgment—not so much of general injustice and false judgment, which it has practiced generally in all its works. No, my rebuke is due much more to the particular injustice and false judgment that it practices at the end, in judging its misery greater than my mercy. This is the sin which is pardoned neither here nor there, because the soul cannot be pardoned that disparages my mercy. Therefore, this last sin is graver to me than all the other sins that the soul has committed. For this reason Judas's despair displeased me more, and was graver to my Son, than his betrayal of him.

"So it is that these are rebuked of their false judgment that their sin is greater than my mercy.

On that account they are punished with the devils and eternally tortured with them.

"And they are rebuked of injustice, because they grieve more over their condemnation than over my displeasure. They do not render to me what is mine, and to themselves what is theirs. For to me, they ought to render love. And to themselves, they ought to render bitterness with contrition of heart, and they do the opposite, because to themselves they give love, pitying themselves and grieving on account of the pain they expect for their sin. So you see that they are guilty of injustice and false judgment, and are punished for the one and the other together.

"Because they disparage my mercy, it is with justice that I send them, along with their cruel servant, sensuality, to the cruel tyrant, the devil, whose servants they made themselves through their own sensuality. And I do this so that, together, they are punished and tormented, as together they have offended me. They are tormented, I say, by my ministering devils, whom my judgment has appointed to torment those who have done evil."

Of the glory of the blessed.

" Similarly, the just soul, for whom life ends in the affection of charity and the bonds of love, cannot increase in virtue, time having come to an end. But it can always love with the affection with which it comes to me, and that measure is measured to it. It always desires and loves me, and its desire is not in vain—being hungry, it is satisfied; being satisfied, it is hungry. But the tediousness of satiety and the pain of hunger are far from it.

"In love, the blessed rejoice in my eternal vision, participating in that good that I have in myself, everyone according to that measure of love with which they have come to me. Because they have lived in love of me and of their neighbor, they are united together with general and particular love. They rejoice and exult, participating in each other's good with the affection of love, besides the universal good that they also enjoy together.

"And the blessed rejoice and exult with the angels with whom they are placed, according to their various virtues in the world, being all bound in the bonds of love. Also they have a special participation with those whom they loved with particular affection in the world. With this affection they grew in grace and virtue. And in the life everlasting they have not lost their love, but have it still, their love being added to the universal good. And those souls rejoice in me, and in the other souls and in the blessed spirits, seeing and tasting in them the beauty and the sweetness of my love. And their desires forever cry out to me, for the salvation of the whole world.

"So you see that in those bonds of love in which they finished their life, they go on and remain eternally. They are conformed so entirely to my will that they cannot desire except what I desire, because their freewill is bound in the bond of love in such a way that, time failing them, and, dying in a state of grace, they cannot sin anymore.

"These then do not await, with fear, the divine judgment, but with joy. The face of my Son will not seem to them terrible or full of hatred, because they finished their lives in love and affection for me and in goodwill towards their neighbor. So it is, then, that the transformation is not in his face when he comes to judge with my divine majesty, but in the vision of those who will be judged by him. To the damned he will appear with hatred and with justice, and to the saved with love and mercy."

Of the use of temptations, and how every soul in its extremity sees its final place, either of pain or of glory, before it is separated from the body.

"The devil, dearest daughter, is the instrument of my justice to torment the souls who have miserably offended me. And I have set him in this life to tempt and harass my creatures. And I have done this, not for my creatures to be conquered, but that they may conquer, proving their virtue, and receive from me the glory of victory. And no one should fear any battle or temptation of the devil that may come to him, because I have made my creatures strong and have given them strength of will, fortified in the blood of my Son. Neither devil nor creature can move this will, because it is yours, given by me.

"You, therefore, are free agents. As such, you can hold onto your free will or leave it, according as you please. It is a weapon, which, if you place it in the hands of the devil, immediately becomes a knife with which he strikes you and slays you. But if you do not give this knife of your will into the hands of the devil, that is, if you do not consent to his temptations and harassment, you will never be injured by the guilt of sin in any temptation. You will even be fortified by it when the eye of your intellect is opened to see my love, which allowed you to be tempted, so as to arrive at virtue by being tested.

"Now, no one arrives at virtue except through knowledge of self and knowledge of me. Such knowledge is more perfectly acquired in the time of temptation, because then man knows that he is nothing, and is unable to lift off himself the pains and vexations from which he would flee. And he knows me in his will, which is strengthened by my goodness so that it does not yield to these thoughts. He has seen that my love permits these temptations, for the devil is weak, and by himself can do nothing unless I allow him. Through love and not through hatred I let him tempt, so that you may conquer and not be conquered, so that you may come to a perfect knowledge of yourself and of me, and so that virtue may be proved—for it is not proved except by its opposite.

"You see, then, that the devil is my minister to torture the damned in hell, and in this life, to exercise and prove virtue in the soul. Not that it is the intention of the devil to prove virtue in you (for he has no love), but rather to deprive you of it. And this he cannot do if you do not wish it.

"See, then, how great is the foolishness of men in making themselves weak, when I have made them strong, and in putting themselves into the hands of the devil. Know, then, that at the moment of death, having passed their life under the perverse lordship of the devil (not that they were forced to do so, for they cannot be forced, but they voluntarily put themselves into his hands), they await no other judgment than that of their own conscience, and desperately, despairingly, come to eternal damnation. Hell, through their hate, surges up to them in the extremity of death, and before they get there, they take hold of it by means of their lord the devil.

"The righteous, on the other hand, who have lived in charity and died in love, if they have lived perfectly in virtue, are illuminated with the light of faith. With perfect hope in the blood of the Lamb, when the extremity of death comes, they see the good that I have prepared for them and embrace it with the arms of love, holding fast with pressure of love to me, the supreme and eternal Good. And so they taste eternal life before they have left the mortal body, that is, before the soul is separated from the body.

"Others who have passed their lives, and have arrived at the last extremity of death with an ordinary charity (not in that great perfection), embrace my mercy with the same light of faith and hope that those perfect ones had. But, in them, it is imperfect. For, because they were imperfect, they constricted my mercy, although they still counted my mercy greater than their sins.

"However, the wicked sinners do the contrary, for, seeing with desperation their destination, they embrace it with hatred. So it is that neither the one nor the other waits for judgment, but, in departing this life, they receive their place every one of them, and they taste it and possess it before they depart from the body, at the extremity of death. The damned receive their place with hatred and with despair, and the perfect ones with love and the light of faith, and with the hope of the Blood. And the imperfect arrive at the place of purgatory, with mercy and the same faith."

How if the three powers of the soul (intellect, memory, and will) are not united, there cannot be perseverance, without which no man arrives at his end.

"*I* have explained to you that the three steps of the bridge, which is the body of my only Son, are his feet, his side, and his mouth. I will show you now how those three steps are related to the three powers of the soul, which are its intellect, memory, and will. Just as no one who wishes to pass by the bridge and doctrine of my truth can mount one without the other, and the soul cannot persevere except by the union of its three powers.

"There are two goals, and, for the attainment of either, perseverance is needful—they are vice and virtue. If you desire to arrive at life, you must persevere in virtue, and if you would have eternal death, you must persevere in vice. Thus it is with perseverance that those who want life arrive at me who am life, and it is with perseverance that they who taste the water of death arrive at the devil."

An exposition on Christ's words:
"Whosoever thirsts, let him come
to me and drink."

"You were all invited, corporately and individually, by my truth, when he cried in the temple, 'Whosoever thirsts, let him come to me and drink, for I am the fountain of the water of life.' He did not say, 'Go to the Father and drink,' but he said, 'Come to me.' He spoke these words, because in me, the Father, there can be no pain, but in my Son there can be pain. And you, while you are pilgrims and wayfarers in this mortal life, cannot be without pain, because the earth, through sin, brought forth thorns.

"And why did my Son say, 'Let him come to me and drink'? Because whoever follows his doctrine, whether in the most perfect way or by dwelling in the life of common charity, finds the water of life to drink by tasting the fruit of the Blood, through the union of the divine nature with the human nature. And you, finding yourselves in him, find yourselves also in me, who am the Sea of Peace, because I am one with him, and he with me. So you are invited to the fountain of living water of grace.

"It is right for you to keep by him who is made for you a bridge, not being turned back by any contrary wind that may arise, whether winds of prosperity or of adversity. And it is right for you to persevere till you find me, who am the giver of the water of life, through this sweet and loving Word, my only-begotten Son.

"Why did my Son say, 'I am the fountain of living water'? Because he was the fountain that contained me, the giver of the living water, through the union of divine and human nature. Why did he say, 'Come to me and drink'? Because you cannot pass through this mortal life without pain. In me, the divine Father, there can be no pain, but in him, because of his mortal life, there can be pain. Therefore of him I made for you a bridge. No one can come to me except by him, as he told

you in the words, 'No one can come to the
Father except by me.'

"Now you have seen the way to which you
should keep, and how you should keep to it,
namely, with perseverance. Otherwise you shall
not drink from the fountain of living water. Only
through perseverance can you receive the crown
of glory and victory in the life everlasting."

The general method by which every
rational creature can come out of the sea of the
world, and go to the sea of
peace by the holy bridge.

" *I* will now return to the three steps that you
must climb in order to exit from the river
without drowning and attain the living water, to
which you are invited, and to desire my presence
in the midst of you. For on this way which you
should follow, I am in your midst, by grace
reposing in your souls.

"In order to have desire to mount the steps,
you must be thirsty, because only those who
thirst are invited: 'Whosoever thirsts, let him
come to me and drink.'

"One who is not thirsty will not persevere, for
either fatigue will cause him to stop, or pleasure
will. A person who is not thirsty does not care

to carry the vessel with which he may get the water. Neither does he care for the company, and he cannot go alone. So he turns back at the smallest prick of persecution, for he does not love the way. He is afraid because he is alone; if he were accompanied, he would not be afraid. If only he had ascended the three steps, he would not have been alone, and would, therefore, have been secure. You must then be thirsty and gather yourselves together, as it is said, 'two or three or more.'

"Why is it said 'two or three or more'? The number one is excluded, for, unless one has a companion, I cannot be in the midst. This is no indifferent trifle, for one who is wrapped up in self-love is solitary.

"Why is he solitary? Because he is separated from my grace and the love of his neighbor. Being, by sin, deprived of me, he turns to that which is nothing. So a solitary person, that is, one who is alone in self-love, is not mentioned by my Truth and is not acceptable to me. He says, then, 'If there are two or three or more gathered together in my name, I will be in the midst of them.'

"You know that all the commandments of the Law are completely contained in two, and if these two are not observed, then the Law is not observed. The two commandments are to love me above everything, and your neighbor as yourself. These two are the beginning, the middle, and the end of the Law.

"These two commandments cannot be gathered together in my name without three, that is, without the congregation of the powers of the soul: the memory, the intellect, and the will. The memory retains the remembrance of my benefits and my goodness. The intellect gazes into the inexpressible love that I have shown you by means of my only-begotten Son. I have placed him as the object of the vision of your intellect, so that, in him, you behold the fire of my love. The will drives you to love and desire me, who am your end.

"When these virtues and powers of the soul are congregated together in my name, I am in the midst of them by grace. Then one who is full of my love and love of his neighbor suddenly finds himself the companion of many royal virtues.

"It is then that the appetite of the soul is disposed to thirst—thirst, I say, for virtue, the honor of my name, and salvation of souls. His every other thirst is spent and dead, and he then proceeds securely without any servile fear, having ascended the first step of the affection. The affection, stripped of self-love, mounts above itself and above transitory things. Or, if he will still hold, he does so according to my will—that is, with a holy and true fear and a love of virtue.

"He then finds that he has attained to the second step—the light of the intellect. This light is, through Christ crucified, mirrored in heartfelt love of me, for through him have I shown my love to man.

"Man finds peace and quiet when the memory is filled with my love. You know that an empty thing resounds when touched, but not so when it is full. So the memory, being filled with the light of the intellect, and the affection, being filled with love, will not resound with disordinate merriment or with impatience when moved by the tribulations or delights of the world, because they are full of me, who am every good.

"Having climbed the three steps, the seeker after God finds that the three powers of the soul have been gathered together by his reason in my name. And his soul, having gathered together the two commandments, that is, love of me and of one's neighbor, finds itself accompanied by me, who am its strength and security. It walks safely because I am in the midst of it.

"Then he follows on with anxious desire, thirsting after the way of truth, in which way he finds the fountain of the water of life, through his thirst for my honor and his own salvation and that of his neighbor. For without this thirst he would not be able to arrive at the fountain.

"He walks on, carrying the vessel of the heart, emptied of every affection and disordinate love of the world. But emptied, it is immediately filled with other things, for nothing can remain empty. And, being without disordinate love for transitory things, his heart is filled with love of celestial things and sweet divine love, with which he arrives at the fountain of the water of life, and passes through the door of Christ crucified, and tastes the water of life, finding himself in me, the Sea of Peace."

Of the way in which God manifests himself to the soul who loves him.

"Do you know how I manifest myself to the soul who loves me in truth and follows the doctrine of my sweet and loving Word?

"In many, my virtue is manifested in the soul in proportion to its desire. But I also make three special manifestations. The first manifestation of my virtue, that is, of my love and charity in the soul, is made through the Word of my Son, and shown in the blood that he spilled with such fire of love.

"Now this charity is manifested in two ways: first, in general, to ordinary people, that is, to those who live in the ordinary grace of God. It is manifested to them by the many and diverse benefits that they receive from me.

"The second mode of manifestation, which is developed from the first, is peculiar to those who have become my friends in the way mentioned above. It is known through a sentiment of the soul, by which they taste, know, prove, and feel it.

"This second manifestation, however, is in men themselves: They manifest me through the affection of their love. For though I am no acceptor of creatures, I am an acceptor of holy desires, and find myself in the soul according to the precise degree of perfection that it seeks in me.

"Sometimes I manifest myself (and this is also a part of the second manifestation) by endowing men with the spirit of prophecy, showing them the things of the future. This I do in various ways, according to the need I see in the soul itself and in other creatures.

"At other times the third manifestation takes place. I then form in the mind the presence of the Truth, my only-begotten Son, in many ways, according to the will and the desire of the soul. Sometimes it seeks me in prayer, wishing to know my power, and I satisfy it by causing it to taste and see my virtue. Sometimes it seeks me in the wisdom of my Son, and I satisfy it by placing his wisdom before the eye of its intellect, sometimes in the clemency of the Holy Spirit. And then my goodness causes it to taste the fire of divine charity, and to conceive the true and royal virtues, which are founded on the pure love of one's neighbor."

How the soul, after having mounted
the first step of the bridge, should proceed to
mount the second.

"You have now seen how excellent is the state of one who has attained to the love of a friend. Climbing with the foot of affection, he has reached the secret of the heart, which is the second of the three steps figured in the body of my Son. I wish to show you how one becomes a friend and how, from a friend, he grows into a son, attaining to filial love, and how one may know if he has become a friend.

"In the beginning, a man serves me imperfectly through servile fear. But by practice and perseverance, he arrives at the love of delight, finding his own delight and profit in me. This is a necessary stage through which he must pass to attain perfect love. I call filial love perfect because, by it, a man receives his inheritance from me, the eternal Father, and because a son's love includes that of a friend, which is why I told you that a friend grows into a son.

"What means does he take to arrive at that state? I will tell you. Every perfection and every virtue proceeds from charity, and charity is nourished by humility, which results from the knowledge and holy hatred of self, that is, sensuality. To arrive at that state, a man must persevere, and remain in the cellar of self-knowledge. There he will learn my mercy, through the blood of my only-begotten Son, and will draw to himself this love and my divine charity. As he does so, he will extirpate his perverse self-will, both spiritual and temporal.

"In this process he will find himself hiding in his own house, as did Peter, who, after the sin of denying my Son, began to weep. Yet Peter's lamentations were imperfect and they remained so until after the forty days, that is, until after the Ascension.

"When my Truth returned to me, in his humanity, Peter and the others concealed themselves in the house, awaiting the coming of the Holy Spirit whom my Truth had promised them. They remained barred in from fear, because the soul always fears until it arrives at true love. But they persevered in fasting and in humble and continual prayer until they received the abundance of the Holy Spirit. Then they lost their fear, and followed and preached Christ crucified.

"The soul who wishes to arrive at this perfection, after it has risen from the guilt of mortal sin, recognizing it for what it is, begins to weep from fear of the penalty for its sin. Then it rises to the consideration of my mercy, in which contemplation it finds its own pleasure and profit. This is an imperfect state, and I, in order to develop perfection in the soul, after the 'forty days,' that is, after these two states, withdraw myself from time to time, not in grace but in feeling. My Truth showed you this when he said to the disciples, 'I will go and will return to you.'

"Everything that he said was said primarily and in particular to the disciples. But his sayings also referred in general to the whole present and future, that is, to those who should come after. He said, 'I will go and will return to you'; and so it was. For, when the Holy Spirit returned upon the disciples, he did not return alone, but came with my power and the wisdom of the Son, who is one with me. And he came with his own clemency, which proceeds from me the Father, and from the Son.

"Now, as I told you, in order to raise the soul from imperfection, I withdraw myself from her sentiment, depriving her of former consolations. When it was in the guilt of mortal sin, it had separated itself from me. At that time I deprived it of grace through its own guilt, because that guilt had barred the door of its desires. Therefore the sun of grace did not shine, not through its own defect, but through the defect of the creature who bars the door of desire. When the soul knows itself and its darkness, it opens the window and vomits its filth, by holy confession.

"Then I, having returned to the soul by grace, withdraw myself from it by sentiment. And this I do in order to humble it, and cause it to seek me in truth, and to prove it in the light of faith, so that it may come to prudence. Then, if it loves me without thought of self and with lively faith and with hatred of its own sensuality, it rejoices in the time of trouble, deeming itself unworthy of peace and quietness of mind.

"Now comes the second of the three things of which I spoke, that is: how the soul arrives at perfection, and what it does when it is perfect. This is what it does. Though it perceives that I have withdrawn myself, it does not, on that account, look back. Rather, it perseveres with humility in its practices, remaining barred in the house of self-knowledge.

"And continuing to dwell in that house, the soul awaits, with lively faith, the coming of the Holy Spirit—that is, of me, who am the fire of charity. How does the soul await me? Not in idleness, but in watching and continued prayer. And not only does it wait with physical, but also with intellectual watching, that is, with the eye of its mind alert and watching with the light of faith. It extirpates, with hatred, the wandering thoughts of her heart, looking for the affection of my charity, and knowing that I desire nothing but her sanctification, which is certified to it in the blood of my Son.

"As long as the soul's eye watches in this manner, illumined by the knowledge of me and of itself, it continues to pray with the prayer of holy desire, which is a continued prayer. And it also prays with actual prayer, which it practices at the appointed times, according to the orders of holy church.

"This is what the soul does in order to rise from imperfection and arrive at perfection. And it is to this end, namely, that the soul may arrive at perfection, that I withdraw from it, not by grace but by sentiment.

"Once more do I leave the soul, so that it may see and know its defects. And this I do so that, feeling itself deprived of consolation and afflicted by pain, it may recognize its own weakness and learn how incapable it is of stability or perseverance, thus cutting down to the very root of spiritual self-love. This should be the end and purpose of all the soul's self-knowledge: to rise above itself, mounting the throne of conscience and not permitting the sentiment of imperfect love to turn again in its death struggle. Rather, with correction and reproof, it must dig up the root of self-love with the knife of self-hatred and the love of virtue."

ON PRAYER

*Paths that the soul takes to arrive
at pure and generous love.*

When the soul has passed through the doctrine of Christ crucified, with true love of virtue and hatred of vice, and has arrived at the house of self-knowledge and entered into it, it remains, with its door barred, in watching and constant prayer, separated entirely from the consolations of the world. Why does it shut itself in this manner? It does so out of fear, knowing its own imperfections, and also from the desire of arriving at pure and generous love.

"And because the soul sees and knows well that in no other way can it arrive at pure love, with a lively faith it waits for my arrival, through the increase of grace in it.

"How is a lively faith to be recognized? By perseverance in virtue, and by the fact that the soul never turns back for anything, whatever it may be, nor rises from holy prayer, for any reason except (note well) for obedience or charity's sake. For no other reason ought the soul to leave off prayer.

"For, during the time ordained for prayer, the devil is apt to arrive in the soul, causing much more conflict and trouble than when the soul is not occupied in prayer. This he does so that holy prayer may become tedious to the soul. He tempts the soul often with these words: 'This prayer avails you nothing, for you need attend to nothing except your vocal prayers.' He does this so that, becoming wearied and confused in mind, the soul may abandon the practice of prayer. For prayer is a weapon with which the soul can defend itself from every adversary, if it is grasped with the hand of love, by the arm of free choice in the light of the holy faith."

Here, concerning the sacrament of the body of Christ, the complete doctrine is given; and how the soul proceeds from vocal to mental prayer.

"Know, dearest daughter, how, by humble, continual, and faithful prayer, with time and perseverance, the soul acquires every virtue. It should persevere and never abandon prayer, either through the illusion of the devil or its own fragility. That is, it should never abandon prayer either on account of any thought or movement coming from its own body, or on account of the words of any creature. The devil often places himself upon the tongues of creatures, causing them to chatter nonsensically, with the purpose of preventing the prayer of the soul. All of this the soul should pass by, by means of the virtue of perseverance.

"Oh, how sweet and pleasant to that soul and to me is holy prayer, made in the house of knowledge of self and of me. It opens the eye of the intellect to the light of faith and the affections to the abundance of my charity. And my charity was made visible to you through my visible only-begotten Son, who showed it to you with his blood! This blood intoxicates the soul and clothes it with the fire of divine charity, giving it the food of the sacrament which is placed in the inn of the mystical body of the holy church. That is, the food of the body and blood of my Son, wholly God and wholly man, is administered to you by the hand of my vicar, who holds the key of the Blood.

"This is the inn that I mentioned to you, the inn that stands on the bridge to provide food and comfort for the travelers and the pilgrims who pass by the way of the doctrine of my Truth, so they should not faint through weakness.

"This food strengthens little or much according to the desire of the recipient, whether he receives the food sacramentally or virtually. He receives the food sacramentally when he actually communicates with the blessed sacrament. He receives it virtually when he communicates, both by desire for communion and by contemplation of the blood of Christ crucified. It is as if he communicated sacramentally, with the affection of love. For love is to be tasted in the Blood, which, as the soul sees, was shed through love. On seeing this, the soul becomes intoxicated and blazes with holy desire and satisfies itself, becoming full of love for me and for its neighbor.

"Where can this love be acquired? In the house of self-knowledge with holy prayer. There, imperfections are lost, even as Peter and the disciples, while they remained in watching and prayer, lost their imperfection and acquired perfection. By what means is this love acquired? By perseverance seasoned with the most holy faith.

"But do not think that the soul receives such ardor and nourishment from prayer if it prays only vocally, as do many souls whose prayers are words rather than love. Such as these give heed to nothing except to completing psalms and saying many Our Fathers. And once they have completed their appointed tale, they do not appear to think of anything further, but seem to place devout attention and love in mere vocal recitation. But the soul is not required to do this, for, in doing only this, it bears but little fruit, which pleases me but little.

"But if you asked me whether the soul should abandon vocal prayer, since it does not seem to everyone that they are called to mental prayer, I would reply 'No.' The soul should advance by degrees, and I know well that, just as the soul is at first imperfect and afterwards perfect, so also is it with its prayer. It should nevertheless continue in vocal prayer, while it is yet imperfect, so as not to fall into idleness.

"But the soul should not say its vocal prayers without joining them to mental prayer. That is, while the soul is reciting vocal prayers, it should endeavor to elevate its mind in my love, with the consideration of its own defects and of the blood of my only-begotten Son. For in the Blood, it finds the breadth of my charity and the remission of its sins.

"And this the soul should do, so that self-knowledge and the consideration of its own defects should make it recognize my goodness in itself and continue its practices with true humility. I do not wish defects to be considered in particular, but in general, so that the mind may not be contaminated by the remembrance of particular and hideous sins.

"But I do not wish the soul to consider its sins, either in general or in particular, without also remembering the blood and the broadness of my mercy, for fear that otherwise she should be brought to confusion. And together with confusion would come the devil, who has caused it, under the banner of contrition and displeasure of sin. And so it would arrive at eternal damnation, not only because of its confusion, but also through the despair that would come to it, because it did not seize the arm of my mercy. This is one of the subtle devices with which the devil deludes my servants.

"In order to escape from the devil's deceit and to be pleasing to me, you must enlarge your hearts and affections in my boundless mercy, with true humility. You know that the pride of the devil cannot resist the humble mind, nor can any confusion of spirit be greater than the broadness of my good mercy, if the soul will only truly hope in my mercy.

"Once, if you remember rightly, when the devil wished to overthrow you by confusion, wishing to prove to you that your life had been deluded and that you had not followed my will, you did your duty, which my goodness (which is never withheld from one who will receive it) gave you strength to do. You rose, humbly trusting in my mercy, and saying: 'I confess to my Creator that my life has indeed been passed in darkness. But I will hide myself in the wounds of Christ crucified, and bathe myself in his blood. And so shall my iniquities be consumed, and with desire will I rejoice in my Creator.'

"You remember that then the devil fled. And, turning round to the opposite side, he endeavored to inflate you with pride, saying: 'You are perfect and pleasing to God, and there is no more need for you to afflict yourself or to lament your sins.' And once more I gave you the light to see your true path, namely, humiliation of yourself.

"And you answered the devil with these words: 'Wretch that I am, John the Baptist never sinned and was sanctified in his mother's womb. And I have committed so many sins, and have hardly begun to know them with grief and true contrition. For I see who God is, who is offended by me, and who I am, who offend him.'

"Then the devil, not being able to resist your humble hope in my goodness, said to you: 'Cursed that you are, for I can find no way to take you. If I put you down through confusion, you rise to heaven on the wings of mercy, and if I raise you on high, you humble yourself down to hell. And when I go into hell you persecute me, so that I will return to you no more, because you strike me with the stick of charity.'

"The soul, therefore, should season the knowledge of itself with the knowledge of my goodness, and then vocal prayer will be of use to the soul who prays it, and pleasing to me. And from the vocal imperfect prayer, practiced with perseverance, the soul will arrive at perfect mental prayer. But if it simply aims at completing its tale, and, preferring vocal prayer it abandons mental prayer, it will never arrive at it.

"Sometimes the soul will be so ignorant that, having resolved to say so many prayers vocally in order to complete its tale, will abandon my visitation that it feels by conscience, rather than abandon what it had begun. For I visit its mind, sometimes in one way, and sometimes in another. Sometimes I visit it in a flash of self-knowledge or of contrition for sin, sometimes in the broadness of my charity. Sometimes I place before its mind, in various ways, according to my pleasure and the desire of the soul, the presence of my Truth.

"The soul should not abandon my visitation, for, in doing so, it yields to a deception of the devil. The moment it feels its mind disposed by my visitation in the many ways I have told you, it should abandon vocal prayer. Then, once my visitation has passed, if there is time, it can resume the vocal prayers it resolved to say. But if it does not have time to complete them, it ought not on that account to be troubled or suffer annoyance and confusion of mind

"Of course I am not referring to the Divine Office, which clerics and religious are bound and obliged to say under penalty of offending me, for they must, until death, say their office. But if they, at the hour appointed for saying it, should feel their minds drawn and raised by desire, they should arrange so as to say the office before or after my visitation. Thus they will assure that the debt of rendering the office is not omitted.

"But in any other case, vocal prayer should be abandoned immediately for my visitation. Vocal prayer, made in the way that I have told you, will enable the soul to arrive at perfection. Therefore, the soul should not abandon it, but use it in the way that I have told you.

"And so, with practice in perseverance, the soul will in truth taste prayer, and the food of the blood of my only-begotten Son. Therefore I told you that some communicate virtually with the body and blood of Christ, although not sacramentally. That is, they communicate in the affection of charity, which they taste by means of holy prayer. They communicate little or much, according to the affection with which they pray. Those who proceed with little prudence and without method taste little, and those who proceed with much, taste much.

"For the more the soul tries to loosen her affection from itself and fasten it in me with the light of the intellect, the more it knows. And the more the soul knows, the more it loves. And, loving much, it tastes much.

"You see, then, that perfect prayer is not arrived at through many words, but through affection of desire, when the soul raises itself to me, knowing itself and my mercy, seasoned the one with the other. Thus the soul will practice mental and vocal prayer together, for, even as the active and contemplative life are one, so are they.

"Now, vocal or mental prayer can be understood in many different ways. For I have told you that a holy desire is a continual prayer, in the sense that a good and holy will disposes itself with desire to the occasion actually appointed for prayer, in addition to the continual prayer of holy desire. Therefore, vocal prayer will be made at the appointed time by the soul who remains firm in a habitual holy will, and sometimes vocal prayer will be continued beyond the appointed time. The length of time will vary accordly as charity commands for the salvation of one's neighbor, if the soul sees him in need. And it will vary according to the soul's own needs, which depend on the state in which I have placed her.

"Each person, according to his condition, ought to exert himself for the salvation of souls. For this exercise lies at the root of a holy will. Whatever he may contribute, by words or deeds, towards the salvation of his neighbor, is virtually a prayer. But keep in mind that it does not replace a prayer which one should make oneself at the appointed season.

"As my glorious standard-bearer Paul said, 'He who ceases not to work ceases not to pray.' It was for this reason that I told you that prayer is made in many ways. That is, actual prayer may be united with mental prayer if it is made with the affection of charity, for charity is itself continual prayer.

"I have now told you how mental prayer is reached by exercise and perseverance, and by leaving off vocal prayer in favor of mental when I visit the soul. I have also spoken to you of common prayer, that is, of vocal prayer in general, made outside of ordained times. And I have spoken to you of the prayers of goodwill, and how every exercise, whether performed in oneself or in one's neighbor, with goodwill, is prayer. The enclosed soul should therefore spur itself on with prayer. And when it has arrived at friendly and filial love, it does so. Unless the soul keeps to this path, it will always remain tepid and imperfect, and will love me and its neighbor only in proportion to the pleasure it finds in my service."

How the soul separates itself from imperfect love, and attains to perfect love, friendly and befitting a son or daughter.

"*Until* now I have shown you in many ways how the soul raises itself from imperfection and attains to perfection. And this it does after it has attained to friendly and filial love. I tell you that it arrives at perfect love by means of perseverance, barring itself into the house of self-knowledge.

"Now, knowledge of self must be seasoned with knowledge of me, lest it bring the soul to confusion. For self-knowledge would cause the soul to hate its own sensitive pleasure and the delight of its own consolations. But from this hatred, founded in humility, it will draw patience. With patience it will become strong against the attacks of the devil, against the persecutions of man, and towards me, when, for its good, I withdraw delight from its mind.

"And if the soul's sensuality, through malevolence, should lift its head against reason, the judgment of conscience will rise against it. With hatred of it, the judgment of conscience will hold out reason against it, not allowing such evil emotions to get by it.

"However, sometimes the soul who lives in holy hatred corrects and rebukes itself, not only for the things that are against reason, but also for things that in reality come from me. This is what my sweet servant St. Gregory meant when he said that a holy and pure conscience makes sin where there was no sin. That is, through purity of conscience the soul sees sin where there is no sin.

"Now the soul who wishes to rise above imperfection should await my providence in the house of self-knowledge, with the light of faith, as did the disciples. For the disciples remained in the house in perseverance, in watching, and in humble and continual prayer, awaiting the coming of the Holy Spirit. The soul should remain fasting and watching, with the eye of its intellect fastened on the doctrine of my truth. And it will become humble because it will know itself in humble and continual prayer and in holy and true desire."

The signs by which the soul knows it
has arrived at perfect love.

"It now remains to tell you how it can be seen that souls have arrived at perfect love: by the same sign that was given to the holy disciples after they received the Holy Spirit. At that time they came forth from the house and fearlessly announced the doctrine of my Word, my only-begotten Son, not fearing pain, but rather glorying in it. They did not mind going before the tyrants of the world, to announce the truth to them for the glory and praise of my name.

"So the soul who has awaited me in self-knowledge receives me, on my return to it, with the fire of charity. In charity, while still remaining in the house with perseverance, it conceives the virtues by affection of love and participates in my power.

"With my power and these virtues, this soul overrules and conquers its own sensitive passions, and through charity it participates in the wisdom of my Son. In wisdom it sees and knows my truth, with the eye of its intellect. And it knows the deceptions of spiritual self-love, that is, the imperfect love of its own consolations. It also knows the malice and deceit of the devil, which he practices on those souls who are bound by that imperfect love.

"Therefore this soul arises with hatred of that imperfection and with love of perfection. And, through this love, which is of the Holy Spirit, it participates in his will, fortifying itself to be willing to suffer pain. Then, coming out of the house through my name, it brings forth the virtues on its neighbor.

"Not that by coming out to bring forth the virtues I mean that the soul leaves the house of self-knowledge. Rather, in the time of its neighbor's need it loses the fear of being deprived of her own consolations, and so it sets out to give birth to those virtues that it has conceived through affection of love.

"The souls who have come forth in this manner have reached the fourth state, which is that of perfect union with me. The two last-mentioned states are united, that is, the one cannot exist without the other. For there cannot be love of me without love of one's neighbor, nor love of the neighbor without love of me."

"How the soul, after it has passed through this life, sees fully the praise and glory of my name in everything."

"Who can see the glory and praise of my name? The soul who has left the body and has reached me, its end, sees it clearly, and, in seeing, knows the truth. Seeing me, the eternal Father, it loves. And loving, it is satisfied. Satisfied, it knows the truth, and its will is stayed in my will, bound and made stable. Therefore in nothing can it suffer pain, because it has what it desired to have before it saw me, namely, the glory and praise of my name.

"So now, in truth, this soul sees my glory completely in my saints, in the blessed spirits, and in all creatures and things, even in the devils. And as I told you. And although it also sees the injury done to me, which before caused it sorrow, the injury no longer now can give it pain, but only compassion. And this is because it loves without pain, and prays to me continually, with affection of love, that I will have mercy on the world.

"Pain in this soul is ended, but not love, just as the tortured desire which my Word, the Son, had borne from the beginning when I sent him into the world, ended on the cross in his painful death—but not his love. For if the love that I showed you by means of my Son had terminated and ended then, you would not exist, because by love you are made. And if my love had been drawn back, you could not exist. My love created you, and my love possesses you, because I am one with my Truth, and he, the Word incarnate, is one with me.

"You see, then, that the saints and every soul in eternal life desire the salvation of souls without pain, because pain ended in their death, but not so the affection of love.

"Thus, as if intoxicated with the blood of the immaculate Lamb and clothed in the love of their neighbor, they pass through the narrow gate. There, bathed in the blood of Christ crucified, they find themselves in me, the Sea of Peace. Raised from imperfection, far from satiety, they have arrived at perfection, and are satisfied by every good."

How the soul who finds itself in the unitive state desires infinitely to unite itself to God.

"When I depart from the soul so that the body may return a little to its bodily sentiment, the soul, on account of the union that it had made with me, is impatient in its life. It becomes tired of being deprived of union with me and the conversation of the immortals who render glory to me. And it grows weary of finding itself amid the conversation of mortals, and of seeing them so miserably offending me.

"This vision of offenses against me is the torture that such souls always have. And that torture, along with the desire to see me, renders their life intolerable to them. Nevertheless, as their will is not their own, but becomes one with mine, they cannot desire other than what I desire. Though they desire to come and be with me, they are content to remain with their pain, if I desire them to remain, for the greater praise and glory of my name and the salvation of souls. So in nothing are these souls in discord with my will, but they run their course with ecstatic desire, clothed in Christ crucified, and keeping by the bridge of his doctrine, glorying in his shame and pains.

"As much as these souls appear to be suffering, they are rejoicing, because enduring many tribulations is to them a relief in the desire that they have for death. For oftentimes their desire and their will to suffer pain mitigates the pain caused them by their desire to leave the body.

"These who are in the third state not only endure with patience, but they glory, through my name, in bearing much tribulation. In bearing tribulation they find pleasure, and when I permit to them many tribulations, they rejoice, seeing themselves clothed with the suffering and shame of Christ crucified.

"Therefore if it were possible for these souls to have virtue without toil, they would not want it. They would rather delight in the Cross, with Christ, acquiring virtue with pain, than to obtain eternal life in any other way. Why? Because they are inflamed and steeped in the Blood, where they find the blaze of my charity. For my charity is a fire proceeding from me, ravishing their heart and mind and making their sacrifices acceptable.

"Thus, when the affection behind the intellect is nourished and united with me, the eye of the intellect is lifted up and gazes into my Deity. This is a sight that I grant to the soul, infused with grace, who, in truth, loves and serves me."

How those, who have arrived at the
unitive state, have the eye of their
intellect illuminated by supernatural light,
infused by grace.

"With this light that is given to the eye of the intellect, Thomas Aquinas saw me, and for that reason he acquired the light of much knowledge. Augustine, Jerome, the teachers of the church, and my saints were illuminated by my truth to know and understand my truth in the midst of darkness.

"By my truth I mean the Holy Scripture, which seemed dark because it was not understood. And this was not through any defect of the Scriptures, but of those who heard them and did not understand them. Therefore I sent the light of the Holy Scripture to illuminate men's blind and coarse understanding, and to lift up the eye of their intellect to know the truth. And I, Fire, Acceptor of sacrifices, ravishing away from them their darkness, give them light.

"This was not a natural light, but a supernatural one, so that, though in darkness, men might know the truth. So you see that the eye of the intellect has received supernatural light, infused by grace, by which the teachers and saints knew light in darkness. And of darkness they made light.

"The intellect existed before the Scriptures were formed. Therefore from the intellect came knowledge, because in seeing, they discerned. It was in this way that the holy prophets and fathers understood, they who prophesied of the coming and death of my Son. And it was in this way that the apostles understood, after the coming of the Holy Spirit, who gave them that supernatural light. The evangelists, doctors, professors, virgins, and martyrs were all likewise illuminated by that perfect light. And everyone has had the illumination of this light as he needed it for his salvation or that of others, or for the exposition of the Scriptures.

"The teachers of the holy knowledge had it as they expounded on the doctrine of my truth, the preaching of the apostles, and the Gospels of the evangelists. The martyrs had it, declaring in their blood the most holy faith, the fruit and the treasure of the blood of the Lamb. The virgins had it in the affection of charity and purity.

"To the obedient ones is declared, by this light, the obedience of the Word, showing them the perfection of obedience, which shines in my Truth. And my Truth, for the obedience that I imposed upon him, ran to the opprobrious death of the cross.

"This light is to be seen in the Old and New Testament. In the Old, by it the prophecies of the holy prophets were seen by the eye of the intellect, and known. In the New Testament of the evangelical life, how is the gospel declared to the faithful? By this same light.

"And because the New Testament proceeded from the same light, the new law did not break the old law. Rather, the two laws are bound together. The imperfection of the old law, founded in fear alone, was taken from it by the coming of the Word of my only-begotten Son with the law of love. He completed the old law by giving it love, and replaced the fear of penalty by holy fear. And, to show that he was not a breaker of laws, my Truth said to the disciples: 'I came not to dissolve the law, but to fulfill it.'

"It is almost as if my Truth would say to them, 'The law is now imperfect, but with my blood I will make it perfect, and I will fill it up with what it lacks. I will take away the fear of penalty and found it on love and holy fear.' How was this declared to be the truth? By this same supernatural light, which was and is given by grace to all.

"Now, who will receive this light? Every light that comes from Holy Scripture comes and came from this supernatural light. Ignorant and proud men of science were blind notwithstanding this light, because their pride and the cloud of self-love covered up and put out the light. For that reason they understood the Holy Scripture literally rather than with understanding, and tasted only the letter of it, still desiring many other books.

"Such men do not get to the heart of the Scripture, because they have deprived themselves of the light with which the Scripture is found and expounded. They are annoyed and they murmur, because they find much in Scripture that appears to them gross and idiotic.

"Nevertheless, such men appear to be much enlightened in their knowledge of Scripture, as if they had studied it for long. This is not remarkable, because of course they have the natural light whence proceeds science. But because they have lost the supernatural light, infused by grace, they neither see nor know my goodness, nor the grace of my servants.

"Therefore, I say to you, it is much better to go for counsel for the salvation of the soul to a person of holy and upright conscience, than to a proud man of letters who has learned much knowledge. Such a one can only offer what he has himself, and, because of his darkness, it may appear to you that, from what he says, the Scriptures offer darkness. You will find the opposite with my servants, because they offer the light that is in them, with hunger and desire for the soul's salvation.

"This I have told you, my sweetest daughter, that you might know the perfection of this union-producing state, when the eye of the intellect is ravished by the fire of my charity, in which it receives the supernatural light. With this light the souls in the state of union love me, because love follows the intellect, and the more it knows, the more can it love. So the one feeds the other, and, with this light, they both arrive at the eternal vision of me, in which vision they see and taste me, in truth.

How the light of reason is necessary
to every soul that wishes to
serve God in truth.

*T*hen the eternal God, delighting in the thirst and hunger of that servant, and in the purity of her heart, and the desire with which she longed to serve him, turned the eye of his kindness and mercy upon her, and said— "Best-beloved, dearest and sweetest daughter, my spouse! Rise out of yourself, and open the eye of your intellect to see me, the infinite goodness, and the inexpressible love that I have towards you and my other servants. And open the ear of the desire that you feel towards me, and remember, that if you do not see, you cannot hear. That is, the soul who does not see into my Truth with the eye of its intellect cannot hear or know my Truth. Therefore, so that you may know it better, rise above the feelings of your senses.

"And I, who take delight in your request, will satisfy your demand. Not that you can increase my delight—for I am the cause of you and of your increase of delight, not you of mine. Yet the very pleasure that I take in the work of my own hands causes me delight."

Then that soul obeyed and rose out of herself, in order to learn the true solution of her difficulty. And the eternal God said to her, "So that you may understand better what I shall say to you, I shall revert to the beginning of your request concerning the three lights that issue from me, the true Light. The first is a general light dwelling in those who live in ordinary charity. The other two lights dwell in those who, having abandoned the world, desire perfection.

"You know that, without the light, no one can walk in the truth—that is, without the light of reason. And that light you draw from me, the true light, by means of the eye of your intellect and the light of faith that I have given you in holy baptism— though you may have lost it by your own defects.

For, in baptism, and through the mediation of the blood of my only-begotten Son, you have received the form of faith. You exercise faith in virtue by the light of reason, which gives you life and causes you to walk in the path of truth. By its means you arrive at me, the true light. Without it, you would plunge into darkness.

"It is necessary for you to have two lights derived from this primary light, and to these two I will also add a third. The first lightens you to know the transitory nature of the things of the world, all of which pass like the wind. But this you cannot know thoroughly, unless you first recognize your own fragility. You must know how strong is your inclination, through the law of perversity with which your members are bound, to rebel against me, your Creator. (Not that by this law anyone can be constrained to commit even the smallest sin against his will—but this law of perversity fights lustily against the spirit.)

"I did not impose this law upon you so that my rational creature should be conquered by it, but so he should prove and increase the virtue of his soul. For virtue cannot be proved, except by its opposite.

"Sensuality is contrary to the spirit, and yet, by means of sensuality, the soul is able to prove the love which it has for me, its Creator. How does it prove it? When, with anger and displeasure, she rises against itself. This law has also been imposed in order to preserve the soul in true humility.

"Therefore you see that, while I created the soul to mine own image and likeness, placing it in such dignity and beauty, I caused it to be accompanied by the vilest of all things, imposing on it the law of perversity. I imprisoned it in a body, formed of the vilest substance of the earth, so that, seeing in what its true beauty consisted, it should not raise her head in pride against me. Wherefore, to one who possesses this light, the fragility of his body is a cause of humiliation to the soul, and is in no way matter for pride, but rather for true and perfect humility. So this law does not constrain you to any sin by its strivings, but supplies a reason to make you know yourselves and the instability of the world.

"This should be seen by the eye of the intellect, with the light of holy faith, which is the pupil of the eye. This is the light that is necessary to every rational creature, whatever may be his condition, who wishes to participate in the life of grace, in the fruit of the blood of the immaculate Lamb.

"This is the ordinary light, that is, the light that all persons must possess. For, without it, the soul would be in a state of damnation. This is because the soul, being without the light, is not in a state of grace. For, not having the light, it knows neither the evil of its sin nor the cause of its sin, and therefore cannot avoid or hate it.

"And similarly, if the soul does not know good and the reason for good, that is to say virtue, it cannot love or desire me, who am the essential good. Nor can it love or desire virtue, which I have given you as an instrument and means for you to receive both my grace and myself, the true good.

"See then how necessary is this light, for your sins consist in nothing else than in loving what I hate, and in hating what I love. I love virtue and hate vice. One who loves vice and hates virtue offends me and is deprived of my grace. Such a one walks as if blind, for he knows not the cause of vice, that is, his sensual self-love, nor does he hate himself on account of it. He is ignorant of vice and of the evil which follows it. He is ignorant of virtue and of me, who am the cause of his obtaining life-giving virtue. And he is ignorant of his own dignity, which he should maintain by advancing to grace, by means of virtue. See, therefore, how his ignorance is the cause of all his evil, and how you also need this light."

*Some have placed their desire in the
mortification of the body rather than in the
destruction of their own will; and of the second
light, which is more perfect than the general one.*

"Whhen the soul has arrived at the attainment
of the general light, of which I have
spoken, it should not remain contented. For as long
as you are pilgrims in this life, you are capable of
growth. One who does not go forward, by that
very fact, is turning back. The soul should either
grow in the general light, which it has acquired
through my grace, or strive anxiously to attain to
the second and perfect light. For, if the soul truly
has light, it will wish to arrive at perfection.

"In this second, perfect light are to be found
two kinds of perfection. One perfection is that
of those who give themselves up wholly to the
castigation of the body, doing great and severe
penance. These, so that their sensuality may not
rebel against their reason, have placed their
desire in the mortification of the body rather
than in the destruction of their self-will. They
feed their souls at the table of penance, and are
good and perfect. And this is true provided
that they act with true knowledge of themselves and of me, with great humility, and

wholly conformed to the judgment of my will, and not to that of the will of man.

"But, if such souls were not clothed with my will, in true humility, they would often offend against their own perfection, esteeming themselves the judges of those who do not walk in the same path. Do you know why this would happen to them? Because they have placed all their labor and desire in the mortification of the body, rather than in the destruction of their own will. Such as these wish always to choose their own times, and places, and consolations, after their own fashion, and also the persecutions of the world and of the devil.

"They say, cheating themselves with the delusion of their own self-will, which I have already called their spiritual self-will, 'I wish to have that consolation, and not these battles, or these temptations of the devil. Not, indeed, for my own pleasure, but in order to please God the more, and in order to retain him the more in my soul through grace. For it seems to me that I should possess him more, and serve him better in that way than in this.'

"And this is the way the soul often falls into trouble, and becomes tedious and intolerable to itself; thus injuring her own perfection. Yet it does not perceive that within it lurks the stench of pride, and there it lies.

"Now, if the soul were not in this condition, but were truly humble and not presumptuous, it would be illuminated to see that I, the primary and sweet Truth, grant condition, and time, and place, and consolations, and tribulations as they may be needed for your salvation, and to complete the perfection to which I have elected the soul. And it would see that I give everything through love, and that therefore, it should receive everything with love and reverence.

"This is what the souls in the second state do, and, by doing so, they arrive at the third state. I will now speak to you of these souls, explaining to you the nature of these two states which stand in the most perfect light."

Of the third and most perfect state, and of reason, and of the works done by the soul who has arrived at the light.

"Those who belong to the third state, which immediately follows the last, having arrived at this glorious light, are perfect in every condition in which they may be. They receive every event that I permit to happen to them with due reverence. These deem themselves worthy of the troubles and stumbling-blocks that the world causes them, and of the privation of their own consolation, and indeed of whatever circumstance happens to them.

"And inasmuch as these souls deem themselves worthy of trouble, so also do they deem themselves unworthy of the fruit that they receive after their trouble. They have known and tasted in the light my eternal will, which desires nothing but your good. It gives and permits these troubles in order that you should be sanctified in me.

"Therefore the soul, having known my will, clothes itself with it. It fixes its attention on nothing else except seeing in what way it can preserve and increase its perfection to the glory and praise of my name. It opens the eye of her intellect and fixes it in the light of faith upon Christ crucified, my only-begotten Son. It loves and follows his doctrine, which is the rule for the perfect and imperfect alike.

"Then my Truth, the Lamb, who became enamored of this soul when he saw it, gives it the doctrine of perfection. The soul knows what this perfection is, having seen it practiced by the sweet and amorous Word, my only-begotten Son.

"For he was fed at the table of holy desire and sought the honor of me, the eternal Father, and your salvation. Inflamed with this desire, he ran, with great eagerness, to the shameful death of the cross, and accomplished the obedience imposed on him by me, his Father. He shunned neither labors nor insults, nor withdrew on account of your ingratitude or ignorance of so great a benefit. Neither did he withdraw because of the persecutions of the Jews, or on account of the insults, derision, grumbling, and shouting of the people.

"But all this he passed through like the true captain and knight that he was. For I placed him on the battlefield to deliver you from the hands of the devil, so that you might be freed from the most terrible slavery in which you could ever be. And I gave him to you to teach you his road, his doctrine, and his rule, so that you might open the door of me, eternal Life, with the key of his precious blood, shed with such fire of love, with such hatred of your sins.

"It was as if the sweet and loving Word, my Son, had said to you: 'Behold, I have made the road, and opened the door with my blood.' Do not then be negligent to follow. Do not lay down to rest in self-love and ignorance of the road, presuming to choose to serve me in your own way, instead of in the way that I have made straight for you by means of my Truth, the incarnate Word, and built up with his blood. Rise up then, promptly, and follow him, for no one can reach me, the Father, if not by him. He is the way and the door by which you must enter into me, the Sea of Peace.

"When therefore the soul has arrived at seeing, knowing, and tasting this light in its full sweetness, it runs, as one inflamed with love, to the table of holy desire. Like one who has placed his all in this light and knowledge and has destroyed his own will, it shuns no labor, from whatever source it comes. It endures the troubles, the insults, the temptations of the devil, and the murmurings of men. It eats at the table of the most holy Cross, the food of the honor of me, the eternal God, and of the salvation of souls.

"It seeks no reward, either from me or from creatures, because it is stripped of mercenary love, that is, of love for me based on self-interested motives. It is clothed in perfect light and loves me in perfect purity, with no other regard than for the praise and glory of my name. It serves neither me for its own delight, nor its neighbor for its own profit, but purely through love alone.

"Such as these have lost themselves, and have stripped themselves of the Old Man, that is, of their own sensuality. Having clothed themselves with the New Man, the sweet Christ Jesus, my Truth, they follow him manfully.

"These sit at the table of holy desire, having been more anxious to slay their own will than to slay and mortify their own body. They have indeed mortified their body, though not as an end in itself, but as a means to help them keep their own will at bay. Their principal desires should be to slay their own will, so that it may not seek or wish anything else than to follow my sweet Truth, Christ crucified, and to seek the honor and glory of my name and the salvation of souls.

"Those who are in this sweet light know it, and remain constantly in peace and quiet. No one scandalizes them, for they have cut away that thing by which stumbling-blocks are caused, namely, their own will. And all the persecutions, with which the world and the devil can attack them, slide under their feet and do not hurt them. For they remain attached to me by the umbilical cord of fiery desire.

"Such a one rejoices in everything, and does not make himself judge of my servants or of any rational creature. Rather, he rejoices in every condition and in every manner of holiness which he sees, saying: 'Thanks be to you, eternal Father, who have in your house many mansions.'

"And he rejoices more in the different ways of holiness that he sees than if he were to see everyone traveling by one road. He finds, in this way, that he perceives the greatness of my goodness become more manifest. Thus, rejoicing, he draws from all the fragrance of the rose.

"And not only in the case of good, but even when he sees something evidently sinful, he does not fall into judgment. Rather, he shows true and holy compassion and intercedes with me for sinners. And he says, with perfect humility: 'Today it is your turn, and tomorrow it will be mine, unless divine grace preserve me.'

"Dearest daughter, love this sweet and excellent state. Gaze at those who run in this glorious light and holiness, for they have holy minds, and eat at the table of holy desire. They have arrived at feeding on the food of souls, which is the honor of me, the eternal Father. And they are clothed with burning love in the sweet garment of my Lamb, my only-begotten Son, namely, his doctrine. These do not lose their time in passing false judgments, either on my servants or the servants of the world. And they are never scandalized by any murmurings of men, either for their own sake or that of others.

"And since their love is so ordered, these souls, my dearest daughter, never take offense at those they love, nor at any rational creature, for their will is dead and not alive. They never assume the right to judge the will of men, but only the will of my clemency.

"These souls observe the doctrine that was given you by my Truth at the beginning of your life, when you were thinking in what way you could arrive at perfect purity, and were praying to me with a great desire of doing so. You know what I replied to you, while you were asleep, concerning this holy desire. And you know that the words resounded not only in your mind, but also in your ear. So much so, that you returned to your waking body.

"And my Truth said, 'Will you arrive at perfect purity, and be freed from stumbling-blocks, so that your mind may not be scandalized by anything? Unite yourself always to me by the affection of love, for I am the supreme and eternal purity. I am the fire that purifies the soul. The closer the soul is to me, the purer it becomes. And the farther it is from me, the more its purity leaves it.'

"The reason persons of the world fall into such iniquities is that they are separated from me. But the soul who, without any medium, unites itself directly to me, participates in my purity.

"Another thing is necessary for you to arrive at this union and purity, namely, you should never judge the will of man in anything that you may see done or said by any creature whatsoever, either to yourself or to others. You should consider my will alone, both in them and in yourself. And if you should see evidence of sins or defects, draw the rose out of those thorns. That is, offer them to me, with holy compassion.

"In the case of injuries done to you, judge that my will permits them in order to prove virtue in you, and in my other servants. Esteem that one who acts in an injurous manner does so as the instrument of my will. Such apparent sinners may frequently have good intentions, for no one can judge the secrets of the heart of man. What you do not see you should not judge in your mind, even though externally it may be open, mortal sin.

"See nothing in others but my will, not in order to judge, but with holy compassion. In this way you will arrive at perfect purity. For, acting in this way your mind will not be scandalized, either in me or by your neighbor. Otherwise you fall into contempt of your neighbor, if you judge his evil will towards you, instead of acknowledging my will acting in him.

"Such contempt and scandal separates the soul from me and prevents perfection. And, in some cases, it deprives a person of grace, more or less according to the gravity of his contempt and the hatred that his judgment has conceived against his neighbor.

"A different reward is received by the soul who perceives only my will, which wishes nothing else but your good. Everything I give or permit to happen to you, I give so that you may arrive at the end for which I created you. And because the soul remains always in the love of its neighbor, the soul remains always in mine, and thus remains united to me.

"Therefore, in order to arrive at purity, you must entreat me to do three things: First, to grant you to be united to me by the affection of love, retaining in your memory the benefits you have received from me. Second, with the eye of your intellect to see the affection of my love, with which I love you inestimably. And third, in the will of others to discern my will only, and not their evil will. For I am their judge, not you. And in doing this, you will arrive at all perfection.

"This was the doctrine given to you by my Truth. Now I tell you, dearest daughter, that those who have learned this doctrine taste the pledge of eternal life in this life. And, if you have retained this doctrine well, you will not fall into the snares of the devil, because you will recognize them in the case about which you have asked me.

"But nevertheless, in order to satisfy your desire more clearly, I will tell you and show you how men should never discern by judgment, but with holy compassion."

How those who stand in the third and most perfect light receive the pledge of eternal life in this life.

"Why did I say to you that they received the pledge of eternal life? I say that they receive the pledge, but not the full payment, because they wait to receive it in me, who am eternal Life. In me they have life without death, and are filled, but not to excess. In me they have hunger, without pain, for from that divine hunger, pain is far away. Though they have what they desire, their fulfillment contains no excess, for I am the flawless food of life.

"It is true that in this life they receive the pledge and taste it in that the soul begins to hunger for the honor of the eternal God and for the food of the salvation of other souls. And being hungry, it eats. That is, it nourishes itself with love of its neighbor, which causes its hunger and desire. For the love of one's neighbor is a food that never fills to excess the one who feeds on it. Thus the eater cannot be completely filled, and always remains hungry.

"So this pledge is the commencement of a guarantee that is given to mankind. In virtue of this pledge he expects one day to receive his payment. His expectation is not based on the the perfection of the pledge in itself, but on faith, on the certainty which he has of reaching the completion of his being and receiving his payment.

"Therefore this loving soul, clothed in my truth, has already received in this life the earnest of my love, and of its neighbor's. This soul is not yet perfect, but awaits perfection in immortal life.

"I say that this pledge is not perfect, because the soul who tastes it does not yet have the perfection that would prevent its feeling pain in itself, or in others: In itself, through the offense done to me by the law of perversity that is bound in its members and struggles against the spirit; and in others by the offense of its neighbor.

"The soul has indeed, in a sense, a perfect grace. But it does not have that perfection of my saints, those who have arrived at me, who am eternal Life. For their desires are without suffering, and yours are not. These servants of mine, who nourish themselves at this table of holy desire, are both blessed and full of grief, even as my only-begotten Son was, on the wood of the holy cross. There, while his flesh was in grief and torment, his soul was blessed through its union with the divine nature.

"In like manner these servants are blessed by the union of their holy desire towards me. They are clothed in my sweet will. And they are full of grief through compassion for their neighbor, and because they afflict their own self-love, depriving it of sensual delights and consolations."

How this servant of God, rendering thanks, humbles herself; then she prays for the whole world and particularly for the mystical body of the holy church, and for her spiritual children, and for the two fathers of her soul.

*T*hen that servant of God, as if actually intoxicated, seemed beside herself. It was as if the feelings of her body were alienated through the union of love that she had made with her Creator. And it was as if, in elevating her mind, she had gazed into the eternal truth with the eye of her intellect, and, having recognized the truth, had become deeply in love with it.

And she said, "Supreme one! You, supreme and eternal Father, have manifested to me your truth, the hidden deceits of the devil, and the deceitfulness of personal feeling. You have done this so that I, and others in this life of pilgrimage, may know how to avoid being deceived by the devil or ourselves! What moved you to do so? Love, because you loved me, without my having loved you.

"Fire of love! Thanks, thanks be to you, eternal Father! I am imperfect and full of darkness, and you, perfection and light, have shown to me perfection, and the resplendent way of the doctrine of your only-begotten Son.

"I was dead, and you have brought me to life. I was sick, and you have given me medicine. And yours was not only the medicine of the Blood that you gave for the diseased human race in the person of your Son, but also a medicine against a secret infirmity of which I was unaware.

"For you have shown me that, in no way, can I judge any rational creature, and particularly your servants, upon whom I often passed judgment under the pretext of your honor and the salvation of souls. Therefore, I thank you, supreme and eternal good, that, in manifesting your truth, the deceitfulness of the devil, and our own passions, you have made me know my infirmity.

"Therefore I beseech you through grace and mercy that, from today forward, I may never again wander from the path of your doctrine, which was given by your goodness to me and to whoever wishes to follow it. And I beseech you to grant this because without you nothing is done. To you, then, eternal Father, I have recourse and flee.

"I do not beseech you for myself alone, Father, but for the whole world, and particularly for the mystical body of the holy church, that this truth given to me, miserable one that I am, by you, eternal truth, may shine in your ministers.

"Also I beseech you especially for all those whom you have given me, and whom you have made one with me, and whom I love with a particular love. For they will be my refreshment to the glory and praise of your name, when I see them running on this sweet and straight road, pure, and dead to their own will and opinion, and without any passing judgment on their neighbor or causing him any scandal or murmuring. And I pray you, sweetest love, that not one of them may be taken from me by the hand of the infernal devil, so that at last they may arrive at you, their end, eternal Father.

How God renders this soul attentive to prayer, replying to one of her petitions.

*T*hen the eternal God turning the eye of his mercy upon this servant. Not despising her desire, but granting her requests, he proceeded to satisfy the last petition that she had made concerning his promise, saying, "Best beloved and dearest daughter, I will fulfill your desire in this request, so that, on your side, you may not sin through ignorance or negligence. For a fault of yours would be more serious and worthy of graver reproof now than before, because you have learnt more of my truth.

"Apply yourself attentively to pray for all rational creatures, for the mystical body of the holy church, and for those friends whom I have given you, whom you love with particular love. And be careful not to be negligent in giving them the benefit of your prayers, the example of your life, and the teaching of your words, reproving vice and encouraging virtue according to your power.

"Concerning the supports that I have given you, of whom you spoke to me, know that you are truly a means by which they may each receive, according to their needs and fitness. And I, your Creator, grant you this opportunity, for without me you can do nothing. I will fulfill your desires, but do not fail, or they either, in your hope in me. And my providence will never fail you.

So every person, if he is humble, shall receive what he is fit to receive. And every minister shall receive what I have given him to administer, each in his own way, according to what he has received and will receive from my goodness."

How this devout servant, praising and thanking God, made a prayer for the holy church.

Then this servant, as if intoxicated, tormented, and on fire with love, her heart wounded with great bitterness, turned to the supreme and eternal goodness, and said: "Eternal God! Light above every other light! Fire above every fire! You are the only fire that burns without consuming, and consume all sin and self-love found in the soul. You do not afflict the soul, but you fatten it with insatiable love. And though the soul is filled, it is not sated. The more of you it has, the more it seeks. And the more it desires, the more it finds and tastes of you, supreme and eternal fire, abyss of charity.

"Supreme and eternal good, who has moved you, infinite God, to illuminate me, your finite creature, with the light of your truth? You, the same fire of love, are the cause. For it is love that has always constrained and continues to constrain you to create us in your image and likeness, and to show us mercy by giving immeasurable and infinite graces to your rational creatures.

"Goodness above all goodness! You alone are supremely good, and nevertheless you gave the Word, your only-begotten Son, to associate with us filthy ones who are filled with darkness. What was the cause of this? Love. Because you loved us before we were.

"Eternal greatness! You made yourself low and small to make mankind great. On whichever side I turn I find nothing but the abyss and fire of your love. And can a wretch like me pay back to you the graces and the burning love that you have shown and continue to show in particular to me, and the love that you show to all your creatures? No, but you alone, most sweet and loving Father, will be thankful and grateful for me—that is, that the affection of your charity itself will render you thanks. My being, and every further grace that you have bestowed upon me, I have from you. And who gives them to me through love, and not as my due.

"Sweetest Father, when the human race lay sick through the sin of Adam, you sent it a physician, the sweet and loving Word—your Son. And when I was lying infirm with the sickness of negligence and much ignorance, you, most soothing and sweet physician, eternal God, gave a soothing, sweet, and bitter medicine, that I may be cured and rise from my infirmity. You soothed me because with your love and gentleness you manifested yourself to me, sweet above all sweetness. You illuminated the eye of my intellect with the light of most holy faith.

"As it has pleased you to manifest your light to me, I have known the excellence of grace that you have given to the human race. For you administer to it the entire God-Man in the mystical body of the holy church. And I have known the dignity of your ministers, whom you have appointed to administer you to us. I desired that you would fulfill the promise that you made to me, and you gave much more, more even than I knew how to ask for.

"Therefore I know in truth that the human heart does not know how to ask or desire as much as you can give. And thus I see that you are the supreme and eternal good, and that we are not. And because you are infinite, and we are finite, you give what your rational creatures cannot desire enough, filling us with things for which we do not ask you.

"Moreover, I have received light from your greatness and charity, through the love that you have for the whole human race, and in particular for your anointed ones, who ought to be earthly angels in this life. You have shown me the virtue and the blessed state of these your anointed ones, who have lived like burning lamps, shining with the pearl of justice in the holy church.

"And by comparison with these I have better understood the sins of those who live wretchedly. Therefore I have conceived a very great sorrow at offenses done to you, and at the harm done to the whole world. And because you have manifested and grieved over their iniquities—to me, a wretch who am the cause and instrument of many sins—I am plunged into intolerable grief.

"You, inestimable love, have manifested this to me, giving me a sweet and bitter medicine. You have done this so that I might wholly arise out of the infirmity of my ignorance and negligence, knowing myself and your goodness and the offenses that are committed against you. And you have desired that I might shed a river of tears over my wretched self and over those who are dead, in that they live miserably.

"Therefore I do not wish, eternal Father, inexpressible fire of love, that my heart should ever grow weary, or my eyes fail through tears, in desiring your honor and the salvation of souls. But I beg of you, by your grace, that these may be as two streams of water issuing from you, the Sea of Peace.

"Thanks, thanks to you, Father, for granting me what I asked you and what I neither knew nor asked. For by thus giving me matter for grief you have invited me to offer before you sweet, loving, and yearning desires, with humble and continual prayer. Now I beg of you to show mercy to the world and to the holy church. I pray you to fulfill what you caused me to ask you.

"Alas! what a wretched and sorrowful soul is mine, the cause of all these evils. Do not put off any longer your merciful designs towards the world, but descend and fulfill the desire of your servants.

"I know well that mercy is your own attribute, and thus you cannot destroy it or refuse it to one who asks for it. Your servants knock at the door of your truth, because in the truth of your only-begotten Son they know the inexpressible love that you have for mankind. As a result, the fire of your love ought not and cannot refrain from opening to one who knocks with perseverance.

"Therefore, open, unlock, and break the hardened hearts of your creatures, not for their sakes who do not knock, but on account of your infinite goodness. Grant the prayer of those, eternal Father, who, as you see, stand at the door of your truth and pray. For what do they pray? For with the Blood of this door—your Truth— you have washed our iniquities and destroyed the stain of Adam's sin. The blood is ours, for you have made it our bath, and thus you cannot deny it to anyone who truly asks for it.

"Give, then, the fruit of your blood to your creatures. Place in the balance the price of the blood of your Son, so that the infernal devils may not carry off your lambs. You are the good shepherd who, to fulfill your obedience, laid down his life for your lambs, and made for us a bath of his blood.

"That blood is what your hungry servants beg of you at this door. They beg you through it to show mercy to the world, and to cause your holy church to bloom with the fragrant flowers of good and holy pastors, who by their sweet odor shall extinguish the stench of the putrid flowers of sin.

"You have said, eternal Father, that through the love which you have for your rational creatures, and the prayers and the many virtues and labors of your servants, you would show mercy to the world and reform the church, and thus give us refreshment. Therefore do not delay, but turn the eye of your mercy towards us, for you must first reply to us before we can cry out with the voice of your mercy.

"Open the door of your inestimable love which you have given us through the door of your Word. I know indeed that you open before we can even knock. For it is with the affection of love that you have given to your servants, that they knock and cry to you, seeking your honor and the salvation of souls.

"Give them then the bread of life, that is to say, the fruit of the blood of your only-begotten Son, which they ask of you for the praise and glory of your name and the salvation of souls. For more glory and praise will be yours in saving so many creatures than in leaving them obstinate in their hardness of heart.

"To you, eternal Father, everything is possible, and even though you have created us without our own help, you will not save us without it. I beg of you to force their wills, and dispose them to wish for that for which they do not wish. And this I ask you through your infinite mercy.

"You have created us from nothing. Now, therefore, that we are in existence, show mercy to us, and remake the vessels which you have created in your image and likeness. Re-create them to grace in your mercy and the blood of your Son, sweet Christ Jesus."

ON OBEDIENCE

*Where obedience may be found, what
it is that destroys it, what is the sign
of a man's possessing it, and what
accompanies and nourishes it.*

*T*he supreme and eternal Father, kindly
turning the eye of his mercy and clemency
towards his servant, replied: "Your holy desire
and righteous request, dearest daughter, have a
right to be heard. And inasmuch as I am the
supreme Truth, I will keep my word, fulfilling
the promise that I made to you and satisfying
your desire. And if you ask me where obedience
is to be found, and what is the cause of its loss,
and the sign of its possession, I reply that you
will find it in its completeness in the sweet and
loving Word, my only-begotten Son. So prompt
in him was this virtue that, in order to fulfill it,
he hastened to the shameful death of the cross.

"What destroys obedience? Look at the first
man and you will see the cause which destroyed
the obedience imposed on him by me, the eternal
Father. It was pride, which was produced by self-

love, and desire to please his companion. This was the cause that deprived him of the perfection of obedience, giving him instead disobedience, depriving him of the life of grace, and slaying his innocence. As a consequence, he fell into impurity and great misery, and not only he, but the whole human race.

"The sign that you have the virtue of obedience is patience, and impatience is the sign that you do not have it. No one at all can reach eternal life if he does not have the virtue of obedience. For the door to eternal life was unlocked by the key of obedience, which had been fastened by the disobedience of Adam. Then, being constrained by my infinite goodness, since I saw that mankind whom I so much loved did not return to me his end, I took the keys of obedience and placed them in the hands of my sweet and loving Word—the Truth. And he, becoming the porter of that door, opened it.

"No one can enter into eternal life except by means of that door and that porter. That is why he said in the holy gospel that no one could come to the Father, if not by him. When he returned to me, rising to heaven from among mankind at the Ascension, he left you this sweet key of obedience.

"Now I wish you to see and know this most excellent virtue in that humble and immaculate Lamb, and the source whence it proceeds. What caused the great obedience of the Word? The love that he had for my honor and your salvation. Whence proceeded this love? From the clear vision with which his soul saw the divine essence and the eternal Trinity, thus always looking on me, the eternal God.

"His faithfulness obtained this vision most perfectly for him, which vision you imperfectly enjoy by the light of holy faith. He was faithful to me, his eternal Father, and therefore hastened as one in love along the road of obedience, lit up with the light of glory.

"And inasmuch as love cannot be alone, but is accompanied by all the true and royal virtues—because all the virtues draw their life from love—he possessed them all, but in a different way from that in which you do. Among the other virtues he possessed patience, which is the marrow of obedience, and a sign that shows whether a soul is in a state of grace and truly loves or not.

"Consequently, charity, the mother of patience, has given patience as a sister to obedience, and has so closely united them together that one cannot be lost without the other. Either you have them both or you have neither.

"The virtue of obedience has a nurse who feeds it, that is, true humility. Therefore, a soul is obedient in proportion to its humility, and humble in proportion to its obedience.

"Humility is the foster-mother and nurse of charity, and with the same milk it feeds the virtue of obedience. The garments given by this nurse are self-contempt and insult and the desire to displease itself, and to please me.

"Where does it find these attributes? In sweet Christ Jesus, my only-begotten Son. For who abased himself more than he did? He was heaped with insults, jibes, and mockings. He caused pain to himself in his bodily life, in order to please me. And who was more patient than he? for his cry was never heard in murmuring. Rather, he patiently embraced his injuries like one filled with love, fulfilling the obedience imposed on him by me, his eternal Father. As a result, in him you will find obedience perfectly accomplished.

"He left you this rule and this doctrine—which gives you life, for it is the straight way—having first observed them himself. He is the way, and therefore he said, 'I am the way, the truth, and the life.' For one who travels by that way, travels in the light. And being enlightened, he cannot stumble or be caused to fall, without perceiving it. For he has cast from himself the darkness of self-love, by which he fell into disobedience.

"Just as I spoke to you of a companion virtue proceeding from obedience and humility, so I now tell you that disobedience comes from pride, which issues from self-love and deprives the soul of humility. The sister given by self-love to disobedience is impatience, and pride, its foster-mother, feeds her with the darkness of unfaithfulness. So it hastens along the way of darkness, which leads it to eternal death. All this you should read in that glorious book, where you find described this and every other virtue."

How obedience is the key with which heaven is opened, and how the soul should fasten it by means of a cord to her waist.

"Now that I have shown you where obedience is to be found, whence she comes, who is its companion, and who her foster-mother, I will continue to speak of the obedient and of the disobedient together. And I will speak of obedience in general, which is the obedience of the precepts, and in particular, which is that of the counsels. The whole of your faith is founded upon obedience, for by it you prove your faithfulness.

"You are all by my truth to obey the commandments of the law, the chief of which is to love me above everything, and your neighbor as yourself. And the commandments are so bound up together that you cannot observe or transgress one without observing or transgressing all.

"One who observes this principal commandment observes all the others. He is faithful to me and to his neighbor, and is therefore obedient. He becomes subject to the commandments of the law, for my sake. And with humble patience he endures every labor, and even his neighbor's detraction of him.

"Obedience is of such excellence that you all derive grace from it, just as from disobedience you all derive death. Therefore, it is not enough that you should be obedient only in word, and not in practice.

"Obedience is the key which opens heaven, which key my Son placed in the hands of his minister. This minister places it in the hands of everyone who receives holy baptism, promises to renounce the world and all its pomps and delights, and to obey. So everyone has in his own person the very same key that the Word had.

"And if one does not, in the light of faith and with the hand of love, unlock the gate of heaven by means of this key, he never will enter there, in spite of its having been opened by the Word. For though I created you without yourselves, I will not save you without yourselves.

"Therefore you must take the key in your hand and walk by the doctrine of my Word, and not remain seated. That is, you must not place your love in finite things, as do foolish men who follow in Adam's footsteps. Such men cast the key of obedience into the mud of impurity, break it with the hammer of pride, and rust it with self-love.

"This key would have been entirely destroyed had not my only-begotten Son, the Word, come and taken the key of obedience in his hands and purified it in the fire of divine love. For he drew it out of the mud, cleansed it with his blood, straightened it with the knife of justice, and hammered your iniquities into shape on the anvil of his own body. So perfectly did he repair it that no matter how much one may have spoiled his key by his freewill, by the very same freewill, assisted by my grace, he can repair it with the same instruments that were used by my Word.

"Oh! blinder than the blind! Having spoiled the key of obedience, you do not think of mending it!

Do you indeed think that the disobedience that closed the door of heaven will open it? Do you think that the pride that fell can rise? Do you think to be admitted to the marriage feast in foul and disordered garments? Do you think that sitting down and binding yourself with the chain of mortal sin, you can walk? or that without a key you can open the door? Do not imagine that you can, for it is a fantastic delusion.

"You must be firm. You must leave mortal sin through holy confession, contrition of heart, atonement, and the heartfelt intention to amend your life. Then you will throw off that hideous and defiled garment and, clothed in the shining nuptial robe, you will hasten, with the key of obedience in your hand, to open the door.

"But bind this key with the cord of self-contempt and hatred of yourself and of the world, and fasten it to the love of pleasing me, your Creator. And bind this cord tightly to your waist, for fear you lose it.

"Know, my daughter, there are many who take up this key of obedience, having seen by the light of faith that in no other way can they escape eternal damnation. But they hold it in their hand without wearing this belt, or fastening the key to it with the cord of self-contempt. That is to say that they are not perfectly clothed with my pleasure, but still seek to please themselves. They do not wear the cord of self-contempt, for they do not desire to be despised, but rather take delight in the praise of men.

"Such as these are apt to lose their key. For if they suffer a little extra fatigue, or mental or bodily tribulation, and if, as often happens, the hand of holy desire loosens its grasp, they will lose it. They can indeed find it again if they wish to while they live, but if they do not wish, they will never find it. And what will prove to them that they have lost it? Impatience, for patience was united to obedience, and their impatience proves that obedience does not dwell in their soul.

"How sweet and glorious is this virtue of obedience, which contains all the rest, for it is conceived and born of charity. On it is founded the rock of the holy faith. It is a queen whose consort will feel no trouble, but only peace and quiet. The waves of the stormy sea cannot hurt it, nor can any tempest reach the interior of the soul in whom it dwells.

"The obedient one feels no hatred when injured, because he wishes to obey the precept of forgiveness. He does not suffer when her appetites are not satisfied, because obedience has ordered him to desire me alone. For I can and will satisfy all his desires, if he strips himself of worldly riches. And so in all things which would be too long to relate, one who has chosen obedience, the appointed key of heaven, finds peace and quiet. Oh!

"Blessed obedience! You voyage without fatigue, and reach without danger the port of salvation. You are conformed to my only-begotten Son, the Word, so as not to transgress the obedience of the Word, nor abandon his doctrine. You dwell in the love of your neighbor, being anointed with true humility, which saves you from coveting his possessions, contrary to my will.

"You are even cheerful, for your face is never wrinkled with impatience, but it is smooth and pleasant with the happiness of patience. And even in its fortitude you are great by your long endurance, so long that it reaches from earth to heaven and unlocks the celestial door.

"You are a hidden pearl, trampled by the world, abasing yourself, submitting to all creatures. Yet your kingdom is so great that no one can rule you. For you have come out of the mortal servitude of your own sensuality, which destroyed your dignity. And having slain this enemy with hatred and dislike of your own pleasure, you have re-obtained your liberty."

*The misery of the disobedient and the
excellence of the obedient.*

"All this, dearest daughter, has been done by my goodness and providence. For by my providence the Word repaired the key of obedience.

"But worldly persons, like unbridled horses, without the bit of obedience, go from bad to worse, from sin to sin, from misery to misery, until they finally reach the edge of the ditch of death, gnawed by the worm of their conscience. And though it is true that they can obey the precepts of the law if they will, and repent of their disobedience, it is very hard for them to do so, on account of their long habit of sin.

"Therefore let no one trust in putting off finding the key of obedience to the moment of his death. For although everyone may and should hope as long as he has life, he should not put such trust in this hope as to delay repentance.

"What is the reason for such blindness that prevents them from recognizing this treasure? The cloud of self-love and wretched pride, through which mankind abandoned obedience and fell into disobedience. Being disobedient, they are impatient and in their impatience they endure intolerable pain. For impatience has seduced them from the way of truth, leading them along a way of lies, making them slaves and friends of the devils with whom, unless indeed they amend themselves with patience, they will go to the eternal torments.

"On the contrary, my beloved children, obedient observers of the law, rejoice and exult in my eternal vision with the immaculate and humble Lamb, the Maker, Fulfiller, and Giver of this law of obedience. Observing this law in this life, they taste peace without any disturbance, they clothe themselves in the most perfect peace. In peace, they possess every good without any evil, safety without any fear, riches without any poverty, fulfillment without excess, hunger without pain, light without darkness—one supreme infinite good, shared by all those who taste it truly.

"What has placed them in so blessed a state? The blood of the Lamb, by virtue of which the key of obedience has lost its rust, so that, by the virtue of the blood, it has been able to unlock the door.

"Oh! fools and madmen, delay no longer to come out of the mud of impurity, for you seem like pigs, to wallow in the mire of your own lust. Abandon the injustice, murders, hatreds, rancors, detractions, murmurings, false judgments, and cruelty with which you treat your neighbors. Abandon your thefts and treacheries, and the disordinate pleasures and delights of the world. Cut off the horns of pride, by which amputation you will extinguish the hatred that is in your heart against your neighbors.

"Compare the injuries which you do to me and to your neighbor with those done to you, and you will see that those done to you are but trifles. You will see that remaining in hatred you injure me by transgressing my precept. And you also injure the object of your hate, for you deprive him of your love, whereas you have been commanded to love me above everything, and your neighbor as yourself.

"No gloss has been put upon these command-ments, as if it should have been said, 'If your neighbor injures you, do not love him.' Rather, they are to be taken naturally and simply, as they were said to you by my Truth, who him-self literally observed this rule. Literally also should you observe it, and if you do not, you will injure your own soul, depriving it of the life of grace.

"Take, oh! take, then, the key of obedience with the light of faith. Do not walk any longer in such darkness or cold, but observe obedience in the fire of love, so that you may taste eternal life together with the other observers of the law."

How the truly obedient receive a hundredfold for one, and also eternal life.

"*I*n obedience is fulfilled the saying of the sweet and loving Word, my only-begotten Son, in the gospel when he replied to Peter's demand, 'Master, we have left everything for your love's sake, and have followed you, what will you give us?' My Truth replied, 'I will give you a hundredfold for one, and you shall possess eternal life.' It is as if my Truth had wished to say, 'You have done well, Peter, for in no other way could you follow me. And I, in this life, will give you a hundredfold for one.' And what is this hundredfold, beloved daughter, besides which the apostle obtained eternal life? To what did my Truth refer? To temporal substance?

"Properly speaking, no. Do I not, however, often cause one who gives alms to multiply in temporal goods? In return for what? In return for the gift of his own will. This is the one for which I repay him a hundredfold. What is the meaning of the number a hundred? One hundred is a perfect number, and cannot be added to except by recommencing from the first.

"So charity is the most perfect of all the virtues, so perfect that no higher virtue can be attained except by recommencing at the beginning of self-knowledge, and thus increasing many hundredfold in merit. This is that hundredfold that is given to those who have given me the one, that is, their own will, both in general obedience and in the particular obedience of the religious life.

"And in addition to this hundred you also possess eternal life, for charity alone enters into eternal life, like a mistress of a household bringing with her the fruit of all the other virtues, while the others remain outside. The obedient bring their fruit, I say, into me, the eternal Life, in whom they taste eternal life.

"It is not by faith that they taste eternal life, for they experience in its essence that which they have believed through faith. Nor is it by hope, for they possess that for which they had hoped. And so it is with all the other virtues. It is Queen Charity alone who enters and possesses me, her possessor.

"See, therefore, that these little ones receive a hundredfold for one, and also eternal life. For here they receive the fire of divine charity multiplied by one hundred. And because they have received this hundredfold from me, they possess a wonderful and hearty joy. For there is no sadness in charity, but the joy of it makes the heart large and generous, not narrow or double.

"A soul wounded by this sweet arrow does not appear one thing in face and tongue while its heart is different. It does not serve or act towards its neighbor with dissembling and ambition, because charity is an open book to be read by all. Therefore the soul who possesses charity never falls into trouble or the affliction of sadness, or jars with obedience, but remains obedient until death."

This is a brief repetition of the entire book.

" *I* have now, dearest and best beloved daughter, satisfied from the beginning to the end your desire concerning obedience.

"You made four petitions of me with anxious desire, or rather I caused you to make them in order to increase the fire of my love in your soul. The first you made for yourself, and I have satisfied it, illuminating you with my truth, and showing you how you may know this truth that you desired to know. And I explained to you

how you might come to the knowledge of the
truth through the knowledge of yourself and me,
through the light of faith.

"The second request you made of me was that
I should do mercy to the world.

"In the third you prayed for the mystical body
of the holy church, that I would remove darkness
and persecutions from it, punishing its iniquities
in your person. As to this I explained that no
penalty inflicted in finite time can atone for a sin
committed against me, the infinite Good, unless it
is united with the desire of the soul and contrition
of the heart. How this is to be done I have
explained to you.

"I have also told you that I wish to show
mercy to the world, proving to you that mercy is
my special attribute. For through the mercy and
the inestimable love which I had for mankind, I
sent to the earth the Word, my only-begotten
Son. And so that you might understand things
quite clearly, I represented him to you under the
figure of a bridge that reaches from earth to
heaven through the union of my divinity with
your human nature.

"I also showed you, to give you further light
concerning my truth, how this bridge is built on
three steps, namely, on the three powers of the

soul. These three steps I also represented to you, under figures of your body—the feet, the side, and the mouth, by which I also figured three states of soul—the imperfect state, the perfect state, and the most perfect state, in which the soul arrives at the excellence of unitive love.

"I have shown you clearly in each state the means of cutting away imperfection and reaching perfection. I have shown you how the soul may know by which road it is walking. And I have shown you the hidden delusions of the devil and of spiritual self-love.

"Speaking of these three states I have also spoken of the three judgments which my clemency delivers. The first in this is life. The second is at death; it is on those who die in mortal sin without hope. Of these I told you that they go under the bridge by the devil's road, when I spoke to you of their wretchedness. And the third is that of the last and universal judgment.

"And I told you somewhat of the suffering of the damned and the glory of the blessed, when all shall have reassumed their bodies given by me. And now again I repeat my promise, that through the long endurance of my servants I will reform my bride, the church. Therefore I invite you to endure, myself lamenting with you over her iniquities.

"And I have shown you the excellence of the ministers I have given the church, and the reverence in which I wish seculars to hold them. I have shown you the reason their reverence towards my ministers should not diminish on account of the sins of the latter, and how displeasing to me is such lessening of reverence. And I have spoken to you of the virtue of those who live like angels. And while speaking to you on these subjects, I also touched on the excellence of the sacraments.

"And further wishing you to know of the states of tears and whence they proceed, I spoke to you on the subject and told you that all tears issue from the fountain of the heart, and pointed out their causes to you in order. I told you not only of the four states of tears, but also of the fifth, which germinates death.

"I have also answered your fourth request, that I would provide for the particular case of an individual. I have provided, as you know.

"Beyond this, I have explained my providence to you, in general and in particular. I have shown you how everything is made by divine providence, from the first beginning of the world until the end. My providence gives you and permits everything to happen to you, both tribulations and consolations, whether temporal and spiritual.

"Divine providence grants every circumstance of your life for your good, in order that you may be sanctified in me, and that my truth may be fulfilled in you. That truth is that I created you in order to possess eternal life, and manifested this with the blood of my only-begotten Son, the Word.

"I have also fulfilled your desire and my promise to speak of the perfection of obedience and the imperfection of disobedience. And I have shown you how obedience can be obtained and how it can be destroyed. I have shown it to you as a universal key, and so it is.

"I have also spoken to you of particular obedience, and of the perfect and imperfect, and of those in religion, and of those in the world, explaining the condition of each distinctly to you. I have spoken to you of the peace given by obedience, and the war of disobedience. I have told you how the disobedient man is deceived, showing you how death came into the world by the disobedience of Adam.

"Now I, the eternal Father, the supreme and eternal Truth, give you this conclusion of the whole matter: In the obedience of the only-begotten Word, my Son, you have life, and just as from that first Old Man you contracted the infection of death, so all of you who are willing to take the key of obedience have contracted the infection of the life of the New Man, sweet Jesus, of whom I made a bridge because the road to heaven was broken.

"And now I urge you and my other servants to grieve, for by your grief and humble and continual prayer I will show mercy to the world. Die to the world and hasten along this way of truth, so as not to be taken prisoner if you go slowly. I demand this of you now more than at first, for now I have manifested to you my truth.

"Beware that you never leave the cell of self-knowledge, but in this cell preserve and spend the treasure that I have given you, which is the doctrine of truth founded upon the living stone, sweet Christ Jesus, clothed in light which scatters darkness. With which doctrine clothe yourself, my best beloved and sweetest daughter, in the truth."

How this most devout servant of God, thanking and praising God, makes prayer for the whole world and for the holy church, and commending the virtue of faith brings this work to an end.

*T*hen that servant of God, having seen with the eye of the intellect, and having known, by the light of holy faith, the truth and excellence of obedience, hearing and tasting it with love and ecstatic desire, gazed upon God's divine majesty and gave thanks to him in these words:

"Thanks, thanks to you, eternal Father, for you have not despised me, the work of your hands, nor turned your face from me, nor despised my desires. You, the Light, have not regarded my darkness. You, true Life, have not regarded my living death. You, the Physician, have not been repelled by my grave infirmities. You, the eternal Purity, have not considered the many miseries of which I am full. You, who are the Infinite, have overlooked that I am finite. You, who are Wisdom, have overlooked my folly. Your wisdom, your goodness, your clemency, your infinite good, have overlooked these infinite evils and sins, and the many others that are in me.

"Having known the truth through your clemency, I have found your charity and the love of my neighbor. What has constrained me? Not my virtues, but only your charity.

"May that same charity constrain you to illuminate the eye of my intellect with the light of faith, so that I may know and understand the truth that you have manifested to me. Grant that my memory may be capable of retaining your benefits. Grant that my will may burn in the fire of your charity. Grant that that fire may so work in me that I may give my body even to the shedding of blood. Grant that by that blood given for love of the Blood, together with the key of obedience, I may unlock the door of heaven. I ask this of you with all my heart, for every rational creature, both in general and in particular, in the mystical body of the holy church.

"I confess and do not deny that you loved me before I existed, and that your love for me is inexpressible, as if you were mad with love for your creature. Oh, eternal Trinity! Oh, Godhead, which gave value to the blood of your Son! You, eternal Trinity, are a deep Sea, into which the deeper I plunge the more I find, and the more I find the more I seek. The soul cannot be filled to excess in your abyss, for it continually hungers after you, the eternal Trinity, desiring to see you with light in your light.

"As the deer desires the spring of living water, so my soul desires to leave the prison of this dark body and see you in truth. How long, eternal Trinity, fire and abyss of love, will your face be hidden from my eyes? Melt at once the cloud of my body. The knowledge that you have given me of yourself in your truth constrains me to long to abandon the heaviness of my body, and to give my life for the glory and praise of your name.

"For I have tasted and seen with the light of the intellect in your light, the abyss of you, the eternal Trinity. And I have seen the beauty of your human creature. For, looking at myself in you, I saw myself to be your image, my life being given me by your power, eternal Father. And I saw your wisdom, which belongs to your only-begotten Son, shining in my intellect and my will, and being one with your Holy Spirit, who proceeds from you and your Son, by whom I am able to love you.

"You, eternal Trinity, are my Creator, and I am the work of your hands. And I know, through the new creation that you have given me in the blood of your Son, that you are enamored of the beauty of your workmanship.

"Oh, abyss! Oh, eternal Godhead! Oh, deep Sea! What more could you give me than yourself? You are the fire that ever burns without being consumed; in your heat you consume all the soul's self-love. You are the fire which takes away all cold. With your light you illuminate me so that I may know all your truth. You are that light above all light, which illuminates supernaturally the eye of my intellect, and clarifies the light of faith so abundantly and so perfectly that I see that my soul is alive, and in this light it receives you, the true light.

"By the light of faith I have acquired wisdom in the Word—your only-begotten Son. In the light of faith I am strong, constant, and persevering. In the light of faith I hope; do not let me faint by the way.

"This light, without which I would still walk in darkness, teaches me the road. And for this I said, eternal Father, that you have illuminated me with the light of holy faith.

"Of a truth this light is a sea, for the soul revels in you, eternal Trinity, the Sea of Peace. The water of the sea is not turbid, and causes no fear to the soul, for the soul knows the truth: It is a deep that manifests sweet secrets, so that where the light of your faith abounds, the soul is certain of what it believes.

"This water is a supernatural mirror into which you, the eternal Trinity, bid me gaze. You hold it with the hand of love so that I may see myself, who am your creature. There I am represented in you, and you are represented in me, through the union that you made of your Godhead with our humanity.

"For this light I know represents you to me: You, the supreme and infinite good, blessed and incomprehensible good, inestimable good, beauty above all beauty, wisdom above all wisdom—for you are wisdom itself.

"You, the food of the angels, have given yourself in a fire of love to mankind. You, the garment that covers all our nakedness, feed the hungry with your sweetness.

"Sweet, without any bitterness! Eternal Trinity! In your light, which you have given me with the light of holy faith, I have known the many and wonderful things you have declared to me. You have explained to me the path of supreme perfection, so that I may no longer serve you in darkness, but with light. And you have shown me how I may be the mirror of a good and holy life, and arise from my miserable sins.

"Through my sins I have served you in darkness until now. I have not known your truth and have not loved it. Why did I not know you? Because I did not see you with the glorious light of the holy faith. And because the cloud of self-love darkened the eye of my intellect. But you, the eternal Trinity, have dissipated the darkness with your light.

"Who can attain to your greatness, and give you thanks for such immeasurable gifts and benefits as you have given me in this doctrine of truth? for this doctrine has been a special grace over and above the ordinary graces that you give to your other creatures.

"You have been willing to condescend to my need and to that of your creatures—the need to examine the thoughts and feelings of our heart. Having first given me the grace to ask the question, you reply to it, and satisfy your servant, penetrating me with a ray of grace, so that in that light I may give you thanks.

"Clothe me, clothe me with yourself, eternal Truth, so that I may run my mortal course with true obedience and the light of holy faith. For with that light I feel that my soul is about to become intoxicated afresh."

ABOUT PARACLETE PRESS

Paraclete Press is an ecumenical publisher of books and recordings on Christian spirituality. Our publishing represents a full expression of Christian belief and practice—from Catholic to Evangelical, from Protestant to Orthodox.

Paraclete Press is the publishing arm of the Community of Jesus, an ecumenical monastic community in the Benedictine tradition. As such, we are uniquely positioned in the marketplace without connection to a large corporation and with informal relationships to many branches and denominations of faith.

We like it best when people buy our books from booksellers, our partners in successfully reaching as wide an audience as possible.

Books

Paraclete Press publishes books that show the richness and depth of what it means to be Christian. Although Benedictine spirituality is at the heart of all that we do, we publish books that reflect the Christian experience across many cultures, time periods, and houses of worship.

We publish books that nourish the vibrant life of the church and its people—books about spiritual practice, formation, history, ideas, and customs.

We have several different series of books within Paraclete Press, including the bestselling Living Library series of modernized classic texts; A Voice from the Monastery—giving voice to men and women monastics about what it means to live a spiritual life today; award-winning literary faith fiction; and books that explore Judaism and Islam and discover how these faiths inform Christian thought and practice.

Recordings

From Gregorian chant to contemporary American choral works, our music recordings celebrate the richness of sacred choral music through the centuries. Paraclete is proud to distribute the recordings of the internationally acclaimed choir Gloriæ Dei Cantores, who have been praised for their "rapt and fathomless spiritual intensity" by *American Record Guide*, and the Gloriæ Dei Cantores Schola, which specializes in the study and performance of Gregorian chant. Paraclete is also the exclusive North American distributor of the recordings of the Monastic Choir of St. Peter's Abbey in Solesmes, France, long considered to be a leading authority on Gregorian chant performance.

www.paracletepress.com / 1-800-451-5006

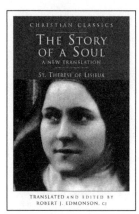